BUILD-A-LAB!
SCIENCE EXPERIMENTS

Astronomy Projects
with an
OBSERVATORY

YOU CAN BUILD

ROBERT GARDNER

Enslow Publishers, Inc.
40 Industrial Road
Box 398
Berkeley Heights, NJ 07922
USA
http://www.enslow.com

Library of Congress Cataloging-in-Publication Data

Gardner, Robert, 1929–
    Astronomy projects with an observatory you can build / Robert Gardner.
        p. cm. — (Build-a-lab science experiments)
    Includes bibliographical references and index.
    ISBN-13: 978-0-7660-2808-1
    ISBN-10: 0-7660-2808-9
    1. Astronomy—Experiments—Juvenile literature. I. Title.
QB46.G329 2007
522—dc22

                            2006032807

Printed in the United States of America

10 9 8 7 6 5 4 3 2 1

To Our Readers: We have done our best to make sure all Internet Addresses in this book were active and appropriate when we went to press. However, the author and the publisher have no control over and assume no liability for the material available on those Internet sites or on other Web sites they may link to. Any comments or suggestions can be sent by e-mail to comments@enslow.com or to the address on the back cover.

Illustration credits: Jonathan Moreno

Photo credits: Enslow Publishers, Inc.

Cover illustrations: Jonathan Moreno (background), © Jupiterimages Corporation (telescope), Shutterstock (moon).

CONTENTS

EXPERIMENTS WITH A 🎗 SYMBOL FEATURE IDEAS FOR YOUR SCIENCE FAIR.

CONTENTS

EXPERIMENTS WITH A 🎗 SYMBOL FEATURE IDEAS FOR YOUR SCIENCE FAIR.

INTRODUCTION

Astronomers **often work at observatories,** where they use giant telescopes to study stars, planets, and distant galaxies. At the Keck Observatory in Mauna Kea, Hawaii, they use a reflecting telescope that has a mirror 10 meters (33 feet) in diameter. But even with the clear skies over Hawaii, astronomers are looking at light that is distorted as it passes through Earth's atmosphere. Better views have been obtained from telescopes in orbit about Earth. For example, the Hubble Space Telescope, which was carried into space by the space shuttle, has provided amazing images of distant parts of the universe.

This book will help you build an observatory of your own that you can use to study the daytime and nighttime sky—a sky unlike that of any other known planet. Your observatory will enable you to carry out experiments and make observations that will answer such questions as the following: Where does Earth fit into the huge universe that surrounds it? Why are there seasons? Why do the Moon and Venus have phases? How many stars can we actually see? How big are the Sun and Moon? and much, much more.

At times, you may need a partner to help you. It would be best if you work with someone who enjoys experimenting as much as you do. In that way you will both enjoy what you are doing. **If any danger is involved in doing an experiment, it will be made known to you. In some cases, to avoid any danger to you, you will be asked to work with an adult. Please do so.** Do not take any chances that could lead to an injury.

Like any good scientist, you will find it useful to record your ideas, notes, data, and anything you can conclude from your experiments in a notebook. By so doing, you can keep track of the information you gather and the conclusions you reach. It will allow you to refer to experiments you have done and will help you in doing other projects in the future.

SCIENCE FAIRS

Some of the experiments in this book contain ideas you might use for a science fair. These projects are indicated with a ♟ symbol. However, judges at science fairs do not reward projects or experiments that are simply copied from a book. For example, a simple diagram or model of the solar system would not impress most judges; however, photographs of a scaled model of the solar system or a yearlong graph and record of the Sun's midday altitude with an explanation of the data would be more likely to attract their attention.

Science fair judges tend to reward creative thought and imagination. It is difficult to be creative or imaginative unless you are really interested in your project; therefore, try to choose an investigation that appeals to you. And before you jump into a project, consider, too, your own talents and the cost of the materials you will need.

If you decide to use an experiment or idea found in this book for a science fair, you should find ways to modify or extend it. This should not be difficult because you will discover that as you do experiments, new ideas come to mind. You will think of experiments that could make excellent science fair projects, particularly because the ideas are your own and are interesting to you.

If you decide to enter a science fair and have never done

so, you should read some of the books listed in the Further Reading section. These books deal specifically with science fairs and will provide plenty of hints and useful information that will help you avoid the pitfalls that sometimes plague first-time entrants. You will learn how to prepare appealing reports that include charts and graphs, how to set up and display your work, how to present your project, and how to talk to judges and visitors.

THE SCIENTIFIC METHOD

When you do a science project, especially one with your own original research, you will need to use what is commonly called the scientific method. In many textbooks you will find a section devoted to the subject. It will probably tell you that the scientific method consists of a series of steps. The book may even list the steps in a particular order.

Many scientists will tell you that there is no set pattern that leads him or her to new knowledge. Each investigation is unique and requires different techniques, procedures, and ways of thinking. Perhaps the best description of the scientific method was given by Nobel-prize-winning physicist Percy Bridgman. He said that the scientific method is doing one's best with one's mind.

The idea that there is a single scientific method that all scientists follow probably came about because of the way scientists report their findings. All good scientific projects try to answer a question, such as "Do we always see the same side of the Moon?" Once you have a question, you will need to form a hypothesis. A hypothesis is an idea of what you think will happen. Perhaps you think we do always see the same side of the moon. Your experiment should then test your hypothesis.

Scientific reports are very similar in format and include the problem, the hypothesis, the experimental procedure, the results, and a conclusion. You will follow a similar format when you prepare the report for your project. The format will include references to authority (searching the litera-ture), coming up with a question, and forming a hypothesis. You will then report your results and any relationships that may lead to a conclusion.

SAFETY FIRST

Most of the projects included in this book are perfectly safe. However, read the following safety rules before you start any project.

1. **Never look directly at the Sun! It can damage your eyes.**

2. Do any experiments or projects, whether from this book or of your own design, under the supervision of a science teacher or other knowledgeable adult.

3. Read all instructions carefully before proceeding with a project. If you have questions, check with your supervisor before going any further.

4. Maintain a serious attitude while conducting experiments. Fooling around can be dangerous to you and to others.

5. Wear approved safety goggles when you are working with a flame or doing anything that might cause injury to your eyes.

6. Have a first-aid kit nearby while you are experimenting.

7. Do not put your fingers or any object other than properly designed electrical connectors into electrical outlets.

8. Never let water droplets come in contact with a hot lightbulb.

9. Never experiment with household electricity.

10. When doing these experiments, use only non-mercury thermometers, such as those filled with alcohol. The liquid in some thermometers is mercury. It is dangerous to breathe mercury vapor, and such thermometers have been banned in many states. If you have a mercury thermometer in the house, **ask an adult** if it can be taken to a local mercury thermometer exchange location.

BUILD YOUR OWN OBSERVATORY

When you think of an astronomer's observatory, you probably picture a dome-shaped building that surrounds a huge telescope. However, people studied and made discoveries about objects in the sky long before Galileo turned his telescope to the Moon and planets. You can repeat some of these pre-telescope discoveries after you build your own simple observatory and use it to learn more about the Sun, Moon, planets, and stars. For the most part, your observatory should be outdoors in an open place where you can see all or most of the sky. If you live in a city, a flat rooftop (if safe), a school playground, or a park may be suitable. Talk to a parent or science teacher about a possible site.

For best results, remember that stars are easiest to see on clear, moonless nights or nights when the Moon rises late. Try to find a place where streetlights do not brighten the sky. Do not despair if you cannot see the stars: You can still perform many experiments in this book that do not involve stars.

The materials you will use to carry out experiments in your observatory should be kept inside in a dry place.

To begin, you need to establish the direction called true north. It is a basic part of any observatory, and you will use it often.

DIRECTION: A BASIC NEED FOR YOUR OBSERVATORY

If you know the direction to the North Pole, you can find all the other directions. To get a general idea of where north is, notice where the Sun sets. If you face the direction in which the Sun set, north will be to your right. There are two ways to find true north. You can use a star or a shadow.

You Will Need

- **a clear night**
- **an open area**
- **a clear day**
- **2 wooden stakes**
- **hammer**
- **metric tape measure or yardstick**
- **small stones**
- **a friend**

Optional:
- **AN ADULT**
- **drill**
- **wide board**
- **pointed sticks**
- **marking pen**
- **bricks or other heavy objects**

FINDING NORTH WITH A STAR

Because Polaris (the North Star) lies almost directly above Earth's North Pole, it can be used to find true north.

1. On a clear night, look for Polaris. First, find the Big Dipper in the northern sky. (If you live in a very southern part of the United States, the Big Dipper may not be visible during the summer.) It is a group of stars that

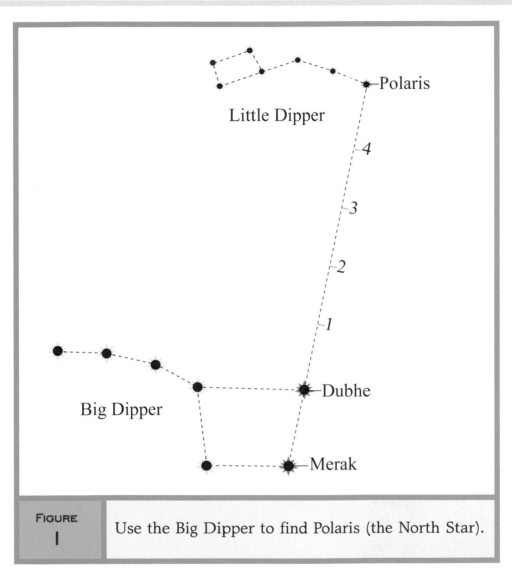

Little Dipper

Polaris

4

3

2

1

Big Dipper

Dubhe

Merak

| FIGURE 1 | Use the Big Dipper to find Polaris (the North Star). |

looks like a dipper (Figure 1). An adult may be able to help
you. The dipper may be turned at a different angle than the
one shown in Figure 1. It may be in any of the positions you
see when you slowly turn Figure 1 all the way around.

2. Merak and Dubhe (see Figure 1) are pointer stars. Hold up your hand and put your thumb and index finger on these two stars in the sky. Imagine a line connecting Merak to Dubhe. Keeping your fingers at the same separation, extend that line five times as far as the distance between Merak and Dubhe. Your finger will be on Polaris. It is the last star on the handle of the Little Dipper.

3. Polaris is almost directly above Earth's North Pole, so the direction we call north is under the North Star. The direction to north is, by definition, 0 degrees (0°). If you face north, east is 90 degrees to your right, the direction your right hand will point if you raise your right arm. South is 180 degrees from north (behind you when you face north). West is 270 degrees, the direction your left hand will point if you raise your left arm while facing north. Another 90 degrees clockwise will bring you back to north—so north can be regarded as 0 degrees or 360 degrees.

   When you find Polaris, establish a sight line to Polaris. Have a partner stand under that sight line. Then, using wooden stakes, mark the point where you are standing and the one where your partner is standing. A line from you to her points toward true north.

A better method that can be used in the daytime when you can see better is explained next.

FINDING NORTH WITH A SHADOW

1. On a clear day, find a flat, open area where you can see all or most of the sky. Hammer a wooden stake into the ground or **ask an adult** to drill a hole in a wide board.

2. Insert one end of a stick that fits into the hole. Be sure the stick is straight up and down. In the northern hemisphere, the stake's or stick's shadow will be shortest when the Sun is directly south of you, at its highest point in the sky. When the Sun is directly south, shadows will point toward true north.

3. You might think that midday, when the Sun is due south, will occur at noon, but this is seldom the case. The best way to find true north is to wait until the Sun is approaching its highest point in the sky. (**Never look directly at the Sun. It can seriously damage your eyes.**) At that time, begin marking the end of the stake's or stick's shadow with small stones,

or with a marking pen if you use a board. Continue to mark it at five-minute intervals until you are certain the shadow is growing longer.

4   Find the shortest shadow by measuring the distances from the stake or stick to the ends of the shadows you marked. Hammer a second stake into the place where you marked the end of the shortest shadow, or have **an adult** drill a second hole and insert another vertical stick if you used a board. A straight line from the first stake or stick to the second will point toward true north (see Figure 2a). In the southern hemisphere, the shortest shadow will point toward true south.

5. If you do not have time to mark shadows at five-minute intervals, mark the end of the stake's or stick's shadow a few minutes before the Sun is highest in the sky. Using the distance between the end of the shadow and the stake or stick as a radius, draw a partial circle around the stake or stick (Figure 2b).

6. When the stick's shadow again touches the circle, mark that point. Draw a straight line connecting the two points on the circle. A line connecting the stake or stick to a point at the

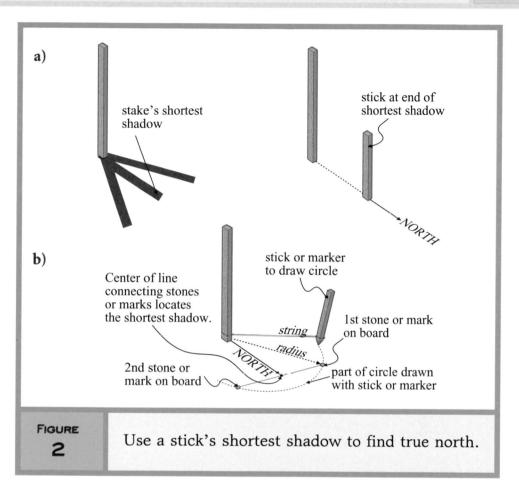

a)

stake's shortest shadow

stick at end of shortest shadow

NORTH

b)

Center of line connecting stones or marks locates the shortest shadow.

stick or marker to draw circle

string

1st stone or mark on board

radius

NORTH

2nd stone or mark on board

part of circle drawn with stick or marker

FIGURE 2	Use a stick's shortest shadow to find true north.

center of the straight line will point toward true north. Insert a second stake or stick at that point. A line from the first stake or stick to the second will point toward true north. How can you find south, east, and west?

If you use a large board, use stones, bricks, or some means of preventing the board from being moved. You will need this north–south line for later experiments.

FINDING NORTH WITH A WATCH AND A STICK

If you have an analog (non-digital) watch, you can make a good estimate of the direction of north.

1. Hold your watch level.

2. Hold a thin stick or toothpick vertically on the center of the watch face.

3. Turn the watch until the stick's shadow lies along the hour hand. North will be approximately halfway between the hour hand and 12 on the watch. Can you explain why?

You Will Need

- **analog watch**
- **thin stick or toothpick**

Hold a magnetic compass above the line you drew that points toward true north. Unless you live along a line stretching from the panhandle of Florida to the western shore of Lake Superior, you will probably find that the compass needle is *not* parallel to the true-north line you drew. Compass needles do not point toward true north (the North Pole) in most places. The reason is that Earth's magnetic pole is in Boothia Peninsula, north of Hudson Bay, about 1,200 miles from Earth's geographic North Pole.

You Will Need

- **north–south line in your observatory**
- **magnetic compass**

BUILDING SOME INSTRUMENTS FOR YOUR OBSERVATORY

Y ou can build **three instruments** for your observatory. Let's get started with an astrolabe.

AN ASTROLABE

The altitude of a star is the angle between the star and your horizon. To measure the altitudes of stars, planets, and the Moon, you can build an astrolabe like the one shown in Figure 3a. When you look at a star through the soda straw, the string will hang along a line. This line marks an angle that measures the star's altitude (Figure 3b).

You Will Need

- **AN ADULT**
- **2 pieces of corrugated cardboard**
- **large protractors**
- **large pin**
- **thin string**
- **paper clip**
- **a weight, such as a heavy washer**
- **soda straw (wide diameter)**
- **clear tape**
- **drill and small drill bit (optional)**

- **common pins**
- **reference objects**
- **circular objects such as cans and medicine vials that vary in diameter from 15 cm (6 in) to 2.5 cm (1 in)**
- **cloth measuring tape**
- **3-in x 5-in file card**
- **scissors**
- **ruler**
- **tape**
- **stick 57.3 cm (22 9/16 inches) long**

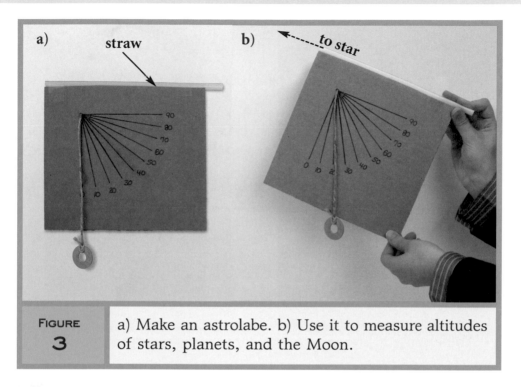

FIGURE
3
a) Make an astrolabe. b) Use it to measure altitudes of stars, planets, and the Moon.

1. To build the astrolabe, you will need a piece of cardboard 20 cm (8 in) on a side. Use a protractor to draw lines to show angles at 10-degree intervals from 0 to 90 degrees (see Figure 3a). You can estimate angles that lie between the lines.

2. Use a large pin to make a hole at the point where the lines meet. Thread a thin string through the hole. Tie one end of the thread to a paper clip on the back side of the cardboard. The paper clip will keep the string in place. Tie the other end to a weight such as a heavy washer.

3. Tape a soda straw with a wide diameter to the edge of the

cardboard. The straw should be parallel to the 90-degree line. When you tip the astrolabe to look at a star through the straw, the string will lie along a line that indicates the star's altitude. Have someone read the angle, or hold your finger against the string so that it does not move when you lower the astrolabe to look at the reading.

AN INSTRUMENT TO MEASURE HORIZONTAL ANGLES

You can use a different instrument to measure azimuths, the angles between distant objects. You will need a piece of thick cardboard about 30 cm (12 in) on a side. Find a large protractor that uses the straight edge of the protractor as its baseline. (Other protractors have the baseline set in a short distance.)

1. Tape the protractor to the cardboard as shown in Figure 4.

2. Stick a small pin into the cardboard at the center of the protractor's baseline.

3. Insert a second pin at the 0-degree mark at one end of the baseline. You will insert a third pin at some point along

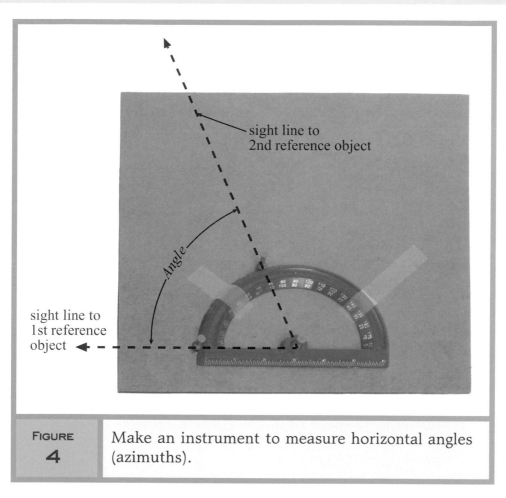

sight line to
2nd reference object

Angle

sight line to
1st reference
object

FIGURE 4	Make an instrument to measure horizontal angles (azimuths).

the curved edge of the protractor. Angles up to 180 degrees can be measured between two points.

4. Take your instrument outside. Sight along the two pins on the baseline to a reference object, such as a tree. Holding the instrument in the same position, look over the center of the baseline toward a second object, such as a sign, post, or

another tree. Insert the third pin at the curved edge of the protractor along this sight line. The two lines of sight, marked by the pins, give the angle between the two objects.

AN INSTRUMENT TO MEASURE SMALL ANGLES

You can build an instrument that will measure small angles—angles less than 10 degrees and even fractions of a degree. Before you do, you need to know something about circles.

1. Gather a number of circular objects that differ in size. For example, you could collect some cans and medicine vials that vary in diameter (distance across their centers) from 15 cm (6 in) to 2.5 cm (1 in).

2. Use a cloth measuring tape to carefully measure the diameter and circumference of (distance around) each circular object. Record all your measurements.

3. For each object, divide its circumference by its diameter. What do you find?

   If you measured carefully, you found that for each object, its circumference divided by its diameter was a number slightly larger than 3. Very careful measurements and advanced mathematics show that this ratio (circumference/diameter) is 3.14159 . . . , a never-ending decimal. This ratio is called pi and is usually represented by the Greek letter π (pi).

$$\frac{\text{Circumference (C)}}{\text{Diameter (D)}} = \pi \text{ (approximately 3.14)}$$

Since the diameter of a circle (D) is also equal to twice the radius (2r), we can also write:

$$\frac{C}{2r} = \pi, \text{ or } C = 2\pi r$$

A protractor, which is half a circle, as you can see, contains 180 degrees. A circle has 360 degrees. Now imagine a circle with a circumference of 360 cm. Each centimeter (cm) on its circumference would be one degree wide when viewed from its center. Since the circumference of a circle is equal to 2π (6.28) times the radius ($C = 2\pi r$), we can find the radius of such a circle. Just divide the circumference by 6.28 (approximately 2π).

$$r = \frac{C}{2\pi} = \frac{360 \text{ cm}}{2\pi} = 57.3 \text{ cm, or } 22.56 \text{ in } (22\tfrac{9}{16} \text{ in})$$

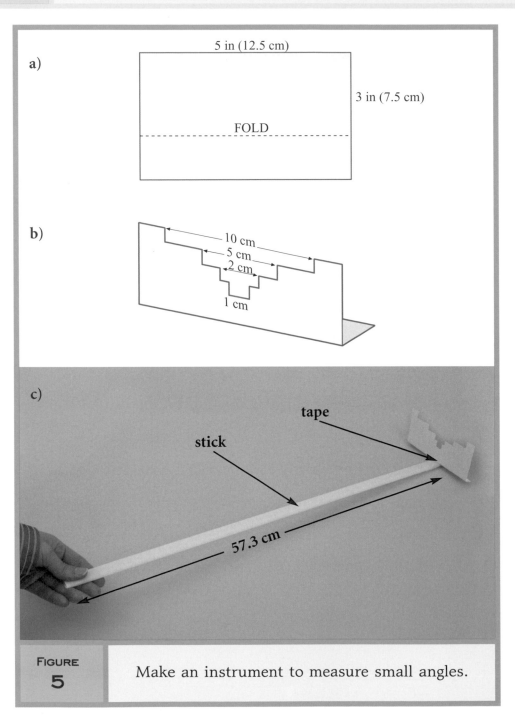

a)

5 in (12.5 cm)

3 in (7.5 cm)

FOLD

b)

10 cm

5 cm

2 cm

1 cm

c)

tape

stick

57.3 cm

FIGURE 5

Make an instrument to measure small angles.

Knowing that radius, you can build an instrument that can be used to measure angles on the celestial spherc (sky).

1. Fold a 3-in x 5-in file card in half, as shown in Figure 5a.

2. Cut out sections that are each 1.0 cm high and 1.0 cm, 2.0 cm, 5.0 cm, and 10.0 cm wide (see Figure 5b).

3. Tape the card to one end of a stick that is 57.3 cm or $22\frac{9}{16}$ inches long, as shown in Figure 5c.

4. Put your eye at the opposite end of the stick from the card. Two stars that are at the edges of the 10-cm slot are 10 degrees apart. Stars at the edges of the 5-cm slot are 5 degrees apart, and so on. You can estimate fractions of a degree for distances of less than a degree.

OTHER MATERIALS

You now have your basic observatory and instruments that you will need to make measurements and find directions. Additional materials needed to do the experiments in the chapters that follow will be listed at the beginning of each experiment.

DIRECTIONS, ANGLES, AND A GLOBAL VIEW OF EARTH

Astronomy involves finding objects in the sky. To locate something, you need to know the direction in which to look for it. You may also need to know its altitude (distance above ground level) in degrees. Your astrolabe will allow you to measure altitudes. You have already determined the direction to true north in your observatory. That gives you a good starting point from which to find other directions.

To locate a star, you need to find its altitude and its azimuth. The star's altitude is the angle of the star above the horizon (eye level). The star's azimuth is its angle from true north.

1. You can make rough measurements of altitude and azimuth by using your fists, as shown in Figure 6. A fist, held at arm's length, covers just about 10 degrees. To confirm this, hold the top of one fist even with the horizon (eye level). Then, counting fists, go up fist on fist until one of your fists is directly over your head. You will have covered 90 degrees, and you probably counted 9 fists to reach that point. Since $90° ÷ 9 = 10°$, you can see that one fist is very nearly 10 degrees.

2. What is the altitude of Polaris in fists? (Estimate fractions of a fist.) What is its approximate altitude in

You Will Need

- **astrolabe built in Chapter 1**

- **bright stars**

- **azimuth-measuring instrument built in Chapter 1**

- **true-north line**

- **partner**

- **stick or marker**

- **pins**

degrees? Its azimuth is very nearly 0 degrees because it is within half a degree of true north. For other stars, you can use the instruments you built to measure horizontal altitudes and azimuths.

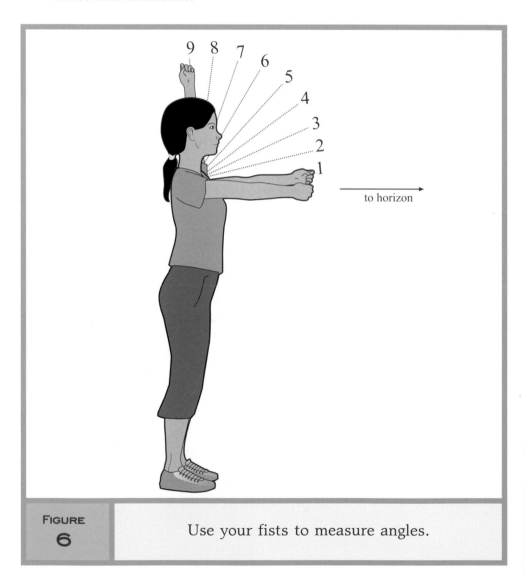

9 8 7 6 5 4 3 2 1

to horizon

FIGURE
6

Use your fists to measure angles.

3. For a more accurate measurement of Polaris's altitude, you can use the astrolabe you built in Chapter 1. Look at Polaris through the soda straw. The weighted string will hang along a line that measures the star's altitude (see Figure 3b). What is the altitude of Polaris? What is Polaris's azimuth?

4. Look for a bright star in the eastern sky. Measure its altitude with both your fists and your astrolabe. How closely do your measurements agree?

5. Measure the same star's azimuth using fists. Then measure its azimuth using the horizontal angle-measuring instrument you built in Chapter 1. To make this measurement accurately and in good light, do the following: Stand over the stick you used to mark the end of the shortest shadow. Ask a partner to stand under the star whose position you are locating. Have the partner use a stick or some other marker to locate where she is standing. The next day you can use the horizontal angle-measuring instrument to find the star's azimuth. It is the angle between the north–south line (the line between the two stakes or sticks used to establish true north) and the line between you and the marker your partner made when she stood under the star.

6. Place the horizontal angle-measuring instrument on top of the northernmost stake or stick used to mark the end of the shortest shadow (see Figure 7).

7. Place a pin at the center of the protractor's base on the line connecting 0 and 180 degrees. Place a second pin at the end of the line at 0°. Line up these two pins with your

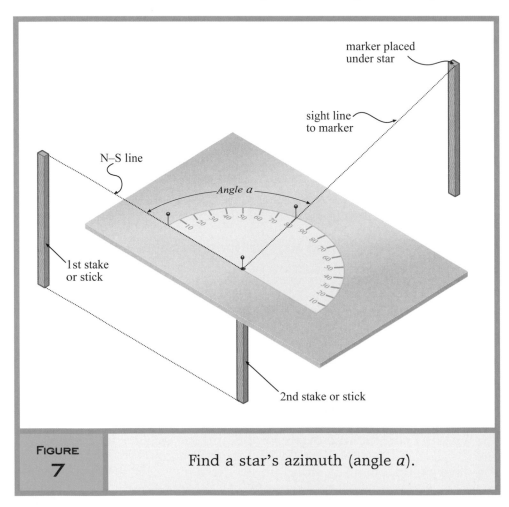

marker placed under star

sight line to marker

N–S line

Angle a

1st stake or stick

2nd stake or stick

| FIGURE 7 | Find a star's azimuth (angle *a*). |

north–south line. The pins now locate a north–south line on the instrument.

8. Have a partner keep these two pins in line with the north–south line. You can then line up a third pin with the stick used to mark the star's position and the pin at the protractor's base. What is the star's azimuth according to this measurement? How closely does it agree with the measurement you made with fists?

9. Repeat your measurements for a star in the western sky. In this case, you will probably find it easier to find its azimuth by measuring its angle west of north. Subtracting the angle you measure from 360° will give you its azimuth. For example, if the star is 90° west of Polaris, its azimuth is 360° – 90° = 270°. (Azimuth is measured clockwise from the reference object, in this case true north.)

A QUESTION TO PONDER

Why do we measure the altitude of clouds in meters (or feet) and the altitude of stars in degrees?

SEPARATION OF STARS AND CONSTELLATIONS

Early astronomers had no idea how far away the stars were. All the stars appeared to be set in the celestial sphere (the apparent dome of the sky) that surrounds Earth. Consequently, they measured stars in terms of the number of degrees in the angles separating stars from one another and from the horizon.

1. You have already found parts of two constellations, the Big Dipper and the Little Dipper. Use an angle-measuring instrument to find the angle between Merak and Dubhe in the Big Dipper (see Figure 1). Once you know that angle, predict the angle between Dubhe and Polaris. Then measure the angle. Was your prediction close to the angle you measured?

   Constellations are groups of stars that form patterns in the sky, such as the Big and Little Dippers. Early astronomers and storytellers liked to imagine they saw star patterns that resembled animals, people, or other things.

   There are several constellations around Polaris. They

You Will Need

- **astrolabe built in Chapter 1**
- **night of bright stars**
- **angle-measuring instrument built in Chapter 1**

are called the polar constellations and are visible at night all year from most of the United States. These constellations include Cassiopeia and Cepheus, as well as Ursa Major (of

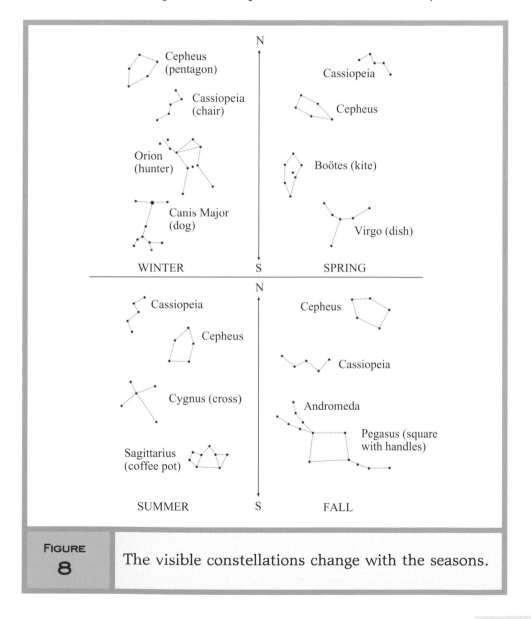

FIGURE
8

The visible constellations change with the seasons.

which the Big Dipper is a part) and Ursa Minor (of which the Little Dipper is a part).

Because Earth orbits the Sun, we see different constellations in much of the sky as the seasons change. The stars we see in winter are on the opposite side of the Sun from the stars we see in summer. Figure 8 shows some of the brightest and easiest-to-find constellations that can be seen during the different seasons.

2. Using an angle-measuring device, find the angles separating stars in one or more of these constellations. Then make a scaled drawing of the constellation or constellations.

EARTH, WHERE WE OBSERVE THE SKY

We determine directions and measure objects in the sky from Earth—our place in this vast universe. But what does Earth look like from space?

In the next experiment, you will see what Earth looks like from a point in space—as it might be seen from the Moon or from another satellite orbiting the third planet from the Sun.

Do this experiment on a sunny day between early April and mid-September, when the Sun is north of the equator.

1. Find a globe of Earth that is about 30 cm (12 in) or more in diameter. Remove it from its stand and place it on a large empty can in your outdoor observatory.

2. Turn the globe so that the town where you live is at the top of the globe. After all, that is the way the world looks to you.

3. Using the north–south line in your observatory, place the globe so that its North Pole is turned toward the north. Use a small piece of clay to hold a toothpick upright on your town on the globe. The toothpick represents you. Its shadow on the globe will point in the same direction as your shadow on the ground.

4. Stand back and look at what you have made—a global view of Earth. It is

You Will Need

- **a globe of Earth about 30 cm (12 in) or more in diameter**
- **large empty can**
- **north-south line in your outdoor observatory**
- **clay**
- **toothpicks**
- **drinking straw**
- **pin**
- **ball**

as if you were looking at Earth from a distant spaceship. What parts of Earth are now in darkness? Along what line is the Sun rising? In what places on Earth is the Sun setting right now? Are there places where there will be sunshine for twenty-four hours? Are there places where there will be darkness for twenty-four hours? What time of day is it now in London? Tokyo? New Delhi? Moscow? New York? San Francisco? Honolulu?

Which way does the Sun seem to be moving around Earth? What happens to the toothpick's shadow as time passes? What happens to your shadow?

5. Where is the Sun directly overhead right now? To find out, cut off a short length of a drinking straw. Stick a pin through the short straw. Move the straw along the globe, keeping it perpendicular to the globe's surface. You will find a place where the Sun shines straight down through the straw and casts no shadow. The Sun must be overhead at this place because it casts no shadow.

6. Where do you think the Sun will be overhead an hour from now? Use the straw to test your prediction an hour later. Were you right?

7. Along what path do you think the Sun will move during an entire day? Test your prediction by locating the overhead midday sun every hour or so. Were you right?

8. Will its path be the same a month from now? If not, how will it differ? Do this experiment a month from now to find out.

9. If the Moon is visible, use a ball to represent it. Place the ball so that it represents the way the Moon looks today. Where would the Moon be relative to the globe if it were a full moon? Where would the Moon be if it were a new moon?

   Keep the globe in place. You will want to use it again after you read about Eratosthenes.

ERATOSTHENES AND EARTH'S SIZE

Eratosthenes (276–194 B.C.) was a Greek astronomer, geographer, and historian who is best known for calculating Earth's circumference. He was living in Alexandria in northern Egypt, which is 31° north of the equator. The city of Syene (now Aswan) was 800 km (500 mi)[1] due south of Alexandria. Eratosthenes had learned that at noon on the first day of summer, the Sun was directly overhead in Syene. He knew this because in Syene on that day, the image of the

---

1. Eratosthenes used a different unit of measurement (stadium). His measurements have been converted to kilometers.

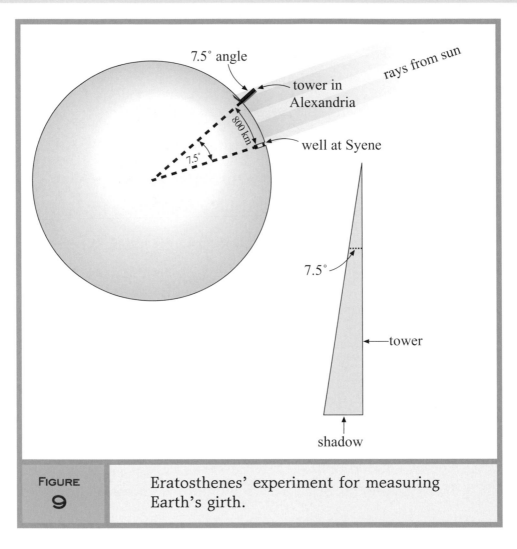

| FIGURE 9 | Eratosthenes' experiment for measuring Earth's girth. |

Sun could be seen reflected from the water in a deep well. At midday, on the first day of summer, knowing that the Sun was directly overhead in Syene, he measured the shadow of a tall pillar in Alexandria. By drawing a triangle, as shown in Figure 9, using the pillar and its shadow as its sides, he found that the Sun's rays made an angle of 7.5 degrees with the pillar. In Syene, 800 km (500 mi) due south, the Sun was overhead at an angle of 0 degrees to any vertical object. Therefore, he reasoned, 800 km along Earth's surface is equivalent to 7.5 degrees of Earth's 360 degrees. Since 7.5 degrees covers 800 km of Earth's circumference, each degree must be equivalent to 107 km, because

$$\frac{800 \text{ km}}{7.5 \text{ degrees}} = 107 \text{ km/degree}$$

Then 360 degrees, or Earth's circumference, must cover

$$360° \text{ x } \frac{107 \text{ km}}{\text{degree}} = 38,520 \text{ km } (23,935 \text{ mi})$$

Eratosthenes' estimate was within 4 percent of Earth's actual circumference, but few people believed he was right. They could not believe Earth was that large because their civilization was limited to the lands around the Mediterranean Sea.

Using your globe and the Sun, you can do an experiment similar to Eratosthenes' and make your own estimate of Earth's circumference.

YOUR MEASUREMENT OF EARTH'S GIRTH

As a model of Eratosthenes' experiment, you can use the globe you used in Experiment 2-3 to measure Earth's circumference.

1. From your local newspaper's weather section or from a weather Internet site, find today's times for sunrise and sunset.

2. Determine the time of midday, which will be midway between sunrise and sunset. To do that, first determine the total time from sunrise to sunset. Divide that time by two and add it to the time of sunrise. For example, suppose the Sun rises at 5:34 A.M. and sets at 6:38 P.M. 6:38 minus 5:34 leaves 13 hours and 4 minutes between sunrise and sunset, or 12 hours and 64 minutes. Half of that time would be 6 hours and

You Will Need

- **globe and other materials from previous experiment**

- **local newspaper or weather Internet site**

- **scissors**

- **tape**

- **measuring tape or flexible ruler**

- **carpenter's level**

- **2 partners**

- **meterstick or yardstick**

- **tape measure (optional)**

- **protractor**

32 minutes. Adding 6 hours and 32 minutes to 5:34 gives 11:66, or, in proper time, 12:06. Midday will occur at 12:06.

3. Use scissors to cut about a 4-cm length from a drinking straw. Stick a pin through the straw.

4. At midday, use the straw to locate where on Earth the Sun is directly overhead as you did in Experiment 2-3. Where is the Sun directly overhead at midday? Mark that point on the globe with a small piece of tape. (If your globe is correctly oriented, the Sun will move along this latitude throughout the day.)

5. Unless the Sun is directly over a latitude line on the globe, you will have to estimate the latitude directly under the Sun. To do this, measure the distance between two latitude lines on the globe with a measuring tape or flexible ruler. Usually they are 10 degrees apart. To find the latitude of a point between two latitude lines, find the position of the point as a fraction of the distance between the lines. For example, on the author's globe, the latitude lines are 2.5 cm apart. If the midday sun is overhead at a point 1.5 cm north of the equator (0° latitude), then its latitude is

$$\frac{1.5 \text{ cm}}{2.5 \text{ cm}} \times 10° = 6.0° \text{ north of the equator}$$

6. While you are locating where the Sun is directly overhead on Earth, have two partners measure the length of the shadow cast by a yardstick or meterstick. One partner should hold the stick in a vertical position. A carpenter's level will help him determine when the stick is vertical. The other partner can mark the end of the stick's shadow and measure both the stick's height and the length of its shadow using a meterstick or a tape measure (Figure 10a). What is the ratio of the length of the shadow to the height of the stick?

7. Use your partner's measurements to make a scaled drawing of the stick and its shadow, as shown in Figure 10b. Use a protractor to measure angle y, shown in Figure 10b, which is the angle the Sun makes with the stick. This is the angle Eratosthenes measured when the Sun shone on the tower at Alexandria.

8. On a large map, use a tape measure or ruler to determine the distance between your latitude and the latitude of the mid-day overhead sun. Most maps have a scale that will allow you to calculate the distance in kilometers or miles. (Remember, 1.6 km = 1 mi.) Once you find the distance between you and

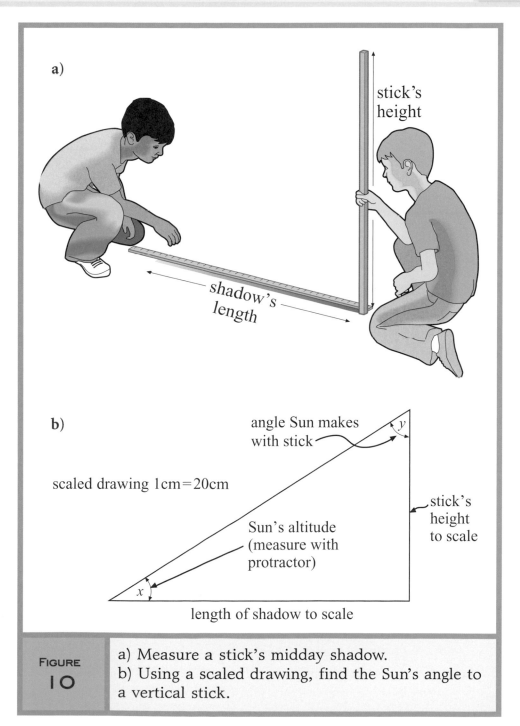

a)

stick's height

shadow's length

b)

angle Sun makes with stick

y

scaled drawing 1cm=20cm

stick's height to scale

Sun's altitude (measure with protractor)

x

length of shadow to scale

FIGURE
10

a) Measure a stick's midday shadow.
b) Using a scaled drawing, find the Sun's angle to a vertical stick.

47

the latitude of the overhead midday sun, you can calculate Earth's circumference just as Eratosthenes did.

What do you calculate Earth's circumference to be? How can you calculate Earth's diameter if you know its circumference? How do your calculations compare with Earth's actual circumference (40,000 km) and diameter (12,756 km)?

IDEAS FOR YOUR SCIENCE FAIR

- Using Eratosthenes' method, find the circumference of the globe you used in this experiment.
- What is the advantage of measuring distances in nautical miles rather than in miles or kilometers?

THE MOON—OUR ONLY NATURAL SATELLITE

Most of the planets that orbit the Sun have natural satellites or moons. Only Mercury is without a moon. Mars has two, Jupiter has sixty-three, Saturn has forty-seven, Uranus has twenty-seven, and Neptune has thirteen. Earth's only natural satellite is our Moon, but we have plenty of human-made satellites orbiting our planet relaying signals or sending data back to Earth.

How Far to the Moon?

Aristarchus of Samos (320–250 B.C.), an early Greek astronomer, estimated the size of the Moon by watching it pass through Earth's shadow during a lunar eclipse. It took 50 minutes for the Moon to completely enter Earth's shadow and 200 minutes to pass all the way through it. Assuming Earth's shadow to have the same diameter as Earth, Aristarchus estimated the Moon's diameter to be one-fourth Earth's diameter (50 ÷ 200 = 0.25, or ¼). Based on Eratosthenes' measurement of Earth's circumference, Aristarchus estimated the Moon's diameter to be 3,120 km. His estimate was quite close for such a crude measurement. More accurate measurements indicate the Moon's diameter to be 3,475 km. Earth's diameter is actually 12,760 km, so the ratio of Moon-to-Earth diameters is 0.27, within 8 percent of Aristarchus's estimate.

Knowing the diameter of the Moon, Aristarchus measured the distance to the Moon. You can do an experiment very similar to his.

You Will Need

- **ruler**
- **scissors**
- **file card**
- **yardstick**
- **a friend**

1. In the middle of a file card, cut a square ¼ inch to a side.

2. Hold a yardstick next to your eye as you look at the Moon. Move the card slowly away from your eye along the yardstick until the diameter of the Moon just fills the ¼-inch width of the square hole in the card. If you can't reach that far, have a friend move the card. How far is the card from your eye?

   As Figure 11 shows, you now have two triangles that are similar. The little one has a base *l* and an altitude *d*; the big one has a base *L* and an altitude *D*. That the two triangles are similar can be proved using geometry. You can assume it to be true because both triangles share a common angle in front of the observer's eye and both are right triangles. Since the triangles are similar, the ratio of their sides is the same. Therefore,

$$\frac{L}{D} = \frac{1}{d} \text{ , and so } L = \frac{l \times D}{d}$$

3. Use your measurements to solve for *L*, the distance to the Moon. For example, suppose you find the Moon's diameter just fits the open square when the square is 29 inches from your eye, then *L*, the distance to the Moon is

$$L = \frac{l \times D}{d} = \frac{29 \text{ in} \times 3{,}475 \text{ km}}{0.25 \text{ in}} = 403{,}100 \text{ km.}$$

Based on your measurements, what do you calculate the distance to the Moon to be?

The Moon's distance from Earth changes. The distance can be measured quite accurately by reflecting radar beams off the Moon. We know that radar pulses travel at the speed of light (300,000 km/s). If it takes 2.7 seconds for a beam to go from Earth to the Moon and back, we know that it takes half of that time—1.35 seconds—to go to the Moon.

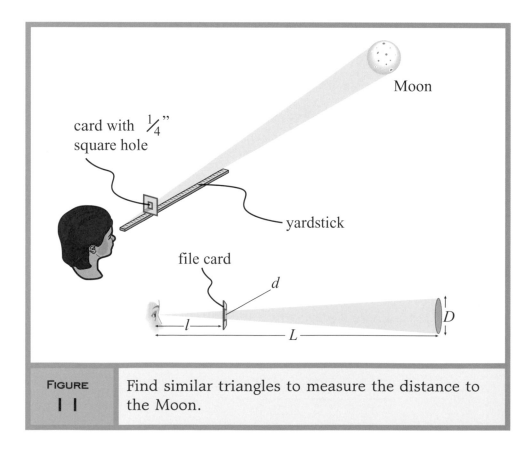

FIGURE	Find similar triangles to measure the distance to
11	the Moon.

Therefore, the Moon's distance from Earth is

300,000 km/s x 1.35 s = 405,000 km (251,600 mi)

The Moon's path (orbit) around Earth is an ellipse (see Figure 20, p. 104), so its distance from Earth changes. The distance 405,000 km (251,600 mi) is the Moon's largest distance from Earth. This largest distance from Earth on the Moon's elliptical orbit is called apogee (*apo* means "away from," *gee* means "Earth"). At perigee ("near Earth"), it is closest to Earth, and a radar beam takes 2.42 seconds to travel to and from the Moon. How far is the Moon from Earth at perigee? What is the Moon's average distance from Earth?

IDEA FOR YOUR SCIENCE FAIR

Hold a file card, whose dimensions you know, perpendicular to the Sun's light. Let its shadow fall on a cardboard screen that is parallel to the file card. How large is the card's shadow? Does the shadow's size change if the screen is moved farther from the card? Why was it reasonable for Aristarchus to assume that Earth's shadow was the same size as Earth? What does this tell you about light rays reaching Earth from the Sun?

OBSERVING THE MOON

1. **The shape of the Moon** seems to change as time passes. A good way to observe these changes is to start with a new moon. Your local newspaper will give the date of a new moon. You can't see a new moon because it is between the Sun and Earth, so none of its reflected light reaches Earth.

2. It will take a day or two before you can see the Moon after a new moon. It will appear as a sliver (crescent) near the setting Sun and will be visible for a short time in the west after the Sun sets.

3. Now that you can see the Moon, keep a record of your observations of the Moon in a notebook. Observe the Moon as often as possible. Record the date and time of each observation and draw the Moon's shape. Whenever possible, measure its distance from the Sun in degrees using fists or one of your angle-measuring instruments. It is perfectly safe to look at the Moon, but **never look directly at the sun.**

You Will Need

- **local newspaper**
- **clear weather**
- **angle-measuring instruments made in Chapter 1**
- **clock or watch**

It can damage your eyes! When you measure the angle between Sun and Moon, cover the Sun with your hand and measure from the edge of your hand.

THE SUN AND MOON AT SUNSET

1. To measure the angle between the Sun and the Moon at sunset, cover the Sun with one of your hands. Then use fists or one of your measuring instruments to find the angle between them. Which side of the Moon (your left or right) is the bright side?

2. Record your measurement along with a drawing, the time, the date, and the Moon's altitude and azimuth. What path does the Moon follow after the Sun sets? Does it follow the path of the Sun? Does it move east or west in the sky?

3. Look for the Moon at about the time of sunset each clear evening for the next two weeks. Take and record the same measurements as before. What happens to the shape of the Moon as days pass? What happens to the angular distance between Moon and Sun as days pass? Is the Moon moving more to the east or to the west of the Sun as days go by? What does this tell you is happening to the time that the Moon

rises? Is it rising earlier, later, or at the same time each day? Have you seen the Moon rising?

LOOKING FOR THE MOON IN DAYTIME

1. After observing the Moon at sunset for a few days, try to find it during the daytime. If you see it, where is it? Record your observations.

2. Look for the rising Moon. Your local newspaper probably includes rising and setting times for both Sun and Moon. Where would you expect to see the Moon rising?

LOOKING FOR THE MOON AFTER SUNSET

1. A full moon rises at about the time that the Sun is setting. Can you explain why? Can you see the Moon at sunset the night after a full moon? On the following night? When can you find the Moon after sunset on these nights? When does the Moon set? What happens to the Moon's setting time as days pass? What happens to the Moon's shape?

2. Approximately how many degrees does the Moon move in one hour? How can you estimate the distance (angle) between Sun and Moon even after the Sun has set?

LOOKING FOR THE MOON IN THE MORNING

1. After the Moon is no longer visible at sunset, begin looking for it early in the morning, before and after sunrise. How is the Moon's shape changing? What is happening to its angular distance from the Sun? Is it east or west of the Sun? Which side of the Moon (your left or right) is the brighter side now? Is this the side nearer to or farther from the Sun?

2. As the days pass, does the Moon move closer to or farther from the Sun? How is this related to the Moon's rising time? What happens to its shape as days pass?

WATCHING THE MOON FOR LONGER TIMES

1. Continue your observations of the Moon for several months. You will begin to see a pattern to its motion and changing appearance. How much time passes between one full moon and the next? Can you explain why the Moon's shape changes the way it does from one new moon to the next?

2. Before you do the next experiment, see if you can make a model to explain the changes in the Moon's appearance from one new moon to the next.

IDEA FOR YOUR SCIENCE FAIR

Try, by observation, to judge the exact time (to the nearest hour) of a half moon (first and last quarter) and a full moon. Then check these times in an almanac. Which is easier to judge, the half or full moon? Why do you think one is easier to judge than the other?

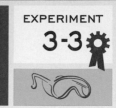
Were you able to design a model to explain the changes in the Moon's appearance from one new moon to the next? If you did, you can compare your model with the one described in this experiment.

All this model requires is a white Styrofoam ball, a toothpick, and the Sun. The best time to observe this model is when the Sun is low in the sky, an hour or two before sunset or after sunrise.

1. In this model, your head represents Earth, the ball represents the Moon, and the Sun is itself. Mount the ball (Moon) on a toothpick. Hold the toothpick supporting the ball so that your hand does not obstruct your view of the ball. Stand with your back to the Sun and support the ball (Moon) at arm's length in front of you and just above your head (Figure 12). You are looking at a "full moon."

2. Slowly rotate your body, moving the "Moon" with you, to your left. Watch its

You Will Need

- **sunny morning or late afternoon**

- **a light-colored ball, about 2–4 inches in diameter (a Styrofoam ball works well)**

- **toothpick**

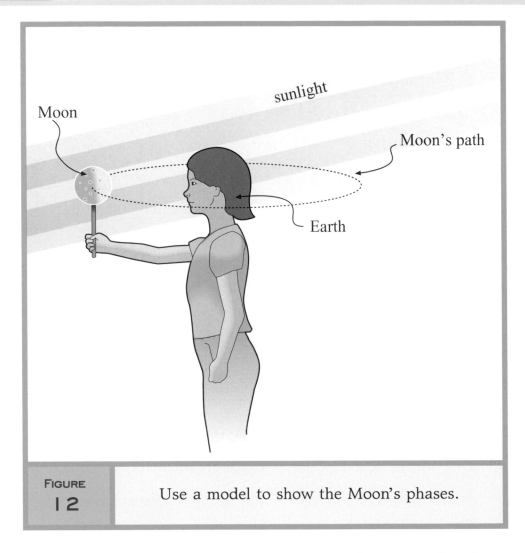

| FIGURE 12 | Use a model to show the Moon's phases. |

lighted part slowly shrink to a half moon (last quarter) and then to a crescent. Cover the Sun with your other hand as you move the Moon across the new moon position (between Earth and Sun). As you continue to move the "Moon" to your left, you will see that a sliver of the Moon nearest the

Sun is lighted—a model of the crescent moon you saw at sunset following a new moon. The lighted part of the Moon increases until only half the Moon is dark (first quarter). As you continue to move the Moon, the lighted portion slowly grows until it becomes a full moon. You have made a complete lunar cycle from one full moon to the next.

If the ball (Moon) were to become covered by the shadow of your head (Earth), what would this represent?

A good model agrees with what we find in the real world. Did this model agree with what you saw in the real world? Did you see the ball's appearance change the way you saw the real Moon change? Did it go from a thin crescent to a half moon, to a full moon, to another half moon (with the opposite side bright), to another crescent (but reversed), and then dark (new moon) as it passed between your head (Earth) and the Sun? If your answers to all these questions were yes, then the model is a good one.

IDEA FOR YOUR SCIENCE FAIR

Make your own model to explain the Moon's phases.

A SCALE MODEL OF EARTH AND THE MOON

B ecause the Moon moves around Earth, it is between Earth and the Sun once a month and behind Earth from the Sun once a month. This may make you wonder why eclipses of the Sun and Moon do not occur on a monthly basis. The reason is that the Moon's orbit is tilted about 5 degrees to the plane of the Sun's orbit. If you build a scale model of Earth and the Moon, you will see why eclipses are infrequent.

You have probably played with toys that are scale models of real things, such as toy cars or dolls. A toy truck that is 10 cm long could be a scale model of a truck that is 10 meters long. The scale for this model truck is 1:100 because:

$$\frac{10 \text{ cm}}{10 \text{ m}} = \frac{10 \text{ cm}}{1000 \text{ cm}} = \frac{1}{100}$$

You Will Need

- **Styrofoam balls with diameters of 1.2–1.3 cm (1/2–5/8 inch) and 5 cm (2 inches)**
- **a stick 1.5 meters or 5 feet long**
- **2 toothpicks**
- **tape**

To make a scale model of Earth and the Moon, you can use what you have learned about the Moon and Earth. The information you will need is given in Table 1.

TABLE I	Information needed to make a scale model of Earth and Moon.		
Object	**Diameter (in km)**	**Diameter (in mi)**	**Average distance of Moon to the Earth**
Moon	3,475	2,160	380,000 km or 240,000 mi
Earth	12,760	7,929	

(The abbreviation for kilometers is km; the abbreviation for miles is mi.)

As you can see, Earth's diameter is almost 4 times larger than the Moon's ($12,760 \div 3,475 = 3.7$). The distance from Earth to the Moon is about 30 times Earth's diameter ($380,000 \div 12,760 = 29.8$).

1. To make a scale model of Earth and the Moon, you can use a Styrofoam ball with a diameter of 1.2–1.3 cm ($\frac{1}{2}$–$\frac{5}{8}$ in) to represent the Moon. Earth can be represented by a Styrofoam ball with a diameter about 4 times as big—about 5 cm (2 in) will do nicely. You will also need a stick 1.5 meters (150 cm) or 5 feet (60 in) long and 2 toothpicks.

2. Tape the toothpicks to opposite ends of the stick and push the balls onto the toothpicks, as shown in Figure 13. The larger ball represents Earth, the smaller ball represents the

Moon. The stick is 150 cm long because Earth and the Moon are about 30 Earth-diameters apart, and 30 x 5 cm = 150 cm (60 inches). The separation of Earth and Moon has the same scale as their diameters. If you wish, you can reduce the scale by half. Make the stick ¾ m (2½ ft) long and use spheres that are 2.5 cm (1 in) and 0.6 cm (¼ in) in diameter.

Why not include the Sun in this model? Well, the Sun's diameter is more than 100 times Earth's diameter, so you would need a lightbulb more than 5 meters (16 ft) wide. Worse yet, the Sun is more than 10,000 Earth-diameters away. To keep the same scale, you would have to place the 5-meter-wide bulb representing the Sun 500 meters (0.3 mi) away from the ball representing Earth.

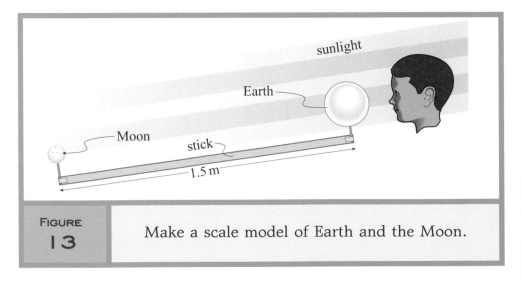

FIGURE 13

Make a scale model of Earth and the Moon.

Since a scale model that includes the Sun is not practical, you can use the real Sun. The Sun's light rays that reach Earth are nearly parallel, so using the real Sun for the model you make is reasonable. The light your model receives would not be very different if you added a scale model of the Sun.

3. Hold the stick so that "Earth" is closer to the Sun, as shown in Figure 13. Place your eye near the ball that represents Earth. Slowly turn the other end of the stick around you. **Remember, never look directly at the sun. It can damage your eyes!** Can you see the different shapes (phases) of the Moon that you saw in the earlier model?

4. Using your scale model, can you see an eclipse of the "Moon"? Tip and turn the stick until Sun, "Earth," and "Moon" are in line. When they are, "Earth's" shadow will fall on the "Moon." By turning the stick slightly, you can see the "Moon" move into and out of "Earth's" shadow.

5. Look closely. Can you see that "Earth's" shadow on the "Moon" is curved? Remember, it was Earth's shadow on the Moon that led Aristarchus to a reasonable estimate of the Moon's diameter. Based on your experimenting with this model, why do you think eclipses are not a monthly occurrence?

DOES A FULL MOON ALWAYS RISE IN THE SAME PLACE?

1. **Look in your newspaper or on the Internet** to find out when you can expect a full moon. From your observatory, watch the full moon rise. In your notebook, record the date, time, and azimuth of the rising Moon.

2. When weather permits, repeat this experiment at the full moon of each lunar cycle for at least a year. Does the full moon always rise in the same place on the horizon every month? If it doesn't, in what month or months does the Moon rise in the southeast and set in the southwest? In what month or months does the Moon rise in the northeast and set in the northwest?

You Will Need

- **daily newspaper or Internet site with information about the Moon**
- **horizontal angle-measuring instrument**
- **north-south line in your observatory**
- **angle-measuring instrument built in Chapter 1**

THE HARVEST MOON

An equinox occurs when the Sun is directly above Earth's equator. There are two equinoxes each year. The vernal (spring) equinox occurs on or about March 21; the autumnal (fall) equinox occurs on or about September 21. The full moon that rises closest to the fall equinox is called a harvest moon. It is called a harvest moon because the Moon rises shortly before or after sunset for several days around the time of the full moon. As a result, farmers have more light than usual in the early evenings, so they can harvest their crops before frost and cold weather arrive.

TIMING THE HARVEST MOON

1. **Use a calendar or almanac** to find the date of the fall equinox (the first day of fall). Then find the date of the full moon closest to the equinox (the harvest moon). Check your daily newspaper or the Internet to find the time of sunset and moonrise for several days before and after the harvest moon. Use a watch or a clock to find the time of sunset and moonrise as you see it. How do your measurements compare with those in the newspaper? Can you explain why they might not be exactly the same?

2. Normally, the Moon rises about 50 minutes later than it did the day before. How much later does the Moon rise each night during the three days before and after the harvest moon?

3. The first full moon after the harvest moon is called the hunter's moon. Does the Moon show a similar rising-time pattern around the time of the hunter's moon?

4. What do you think the rising-time pattern of the Moon would be around the spring (vernal) equinox? Use an almanac to check your prediction. Were you right?

You Will Need

- **calendar or almanac**
- **daily newspaper or Internet weather site**
- **clock or watch**

Is the Moon Really Bigger When It Rises?

If you look at a full moon as it rises, it appears much larger than it does when it is higher in the sky. Is this an illusion?

1. To find out, use the apparatus from Experiment 3-1 (file card with 1/2-inch square opening and yardstick). Look at a full, or nearly full, moon as it rises. Put the end of the yardstick next to your eye. With the file card close to your eye, you can see a lot of sky as well as the Moon. Slide the card along the yardstick and away from your eye. At what distance from your eye does the Moon just fit in the square? If you can't reach this far, have a friend move the card. Record this distance.

2. Later, when the Moon is much higher in the sky, repeat the experiment. At what distance from your eye does the Moon just fit in the square? How does this distance compare with the distance you measured when the Moon was on the horizon? What do you conclude? Is the apparent size of a rising moon an illusion?

You Will Need

- **full moon**

- **apparatus from Experiment 3-1 (file card with ½-inch square opening and yardstick)**

- **a friend**

3. We are actually slightly closer to the Moon when it is high in the sky than when it is rising. Can you explain why?

4. Does the direction we are looking in relation to our body have an effect on our judgment of distance and size? Some scientists think so. Look at a rising full moon as you normally would. Then lean forward so that you have to look up to see the rising moon. Does the Moon appear smaller when you do this?

OUR SUN, THE BIGGEST STAR YOU CAN SEE

Our Sun is the star closest to Earth. While light from most stars takes years to travel to us, the Sun's light reaches us in just a little more than eight minutes. Because light travels at 300,000 kilometers per second, a little arithmetic reveals that the Sun is 150,000,000 kilometers (93,000,000 miles) away. That seems like a huge distance, but light from the next nearest star, Alpha Centauri, takes 4.2 years to reach Earth. That means it is 40 trillion kilometers (25 trillion miles) from Earth. If a spaceship could travel at one-tenth the speed of light (30,000 km/s, or 19,000 mi/s), it would take 42 years to reach Alpha Centauri. For the near future, space travel by humans will be limited to orbits about Earth, the Moon, and, possibly, Mars.

The Sun is so bright that it is the only star you see during daytime. Its brilliance makes it difficult to see any other stars. However, its path across the sky is similar to the path of other stars you see at night. And, just like other stars, the Sun rises and sets. Often its rising and setting paints the sky in bright colors, one of the many beautiful sights in nature.

LOCATING SUNRISE AND SUNSET

1. **Get up in time to see the sunrise.** Using the north–south line in your outdoor observatory and your horizontal angle-measuring instrument, find the azimuth of sunrise. **Do not look directly at the Sun!** Instead, use the shadow of a vertical stick. It will point toward the Sun.

2. Record the azimuth (the angle as measured from true north) of the sunrise and the date in your notebook. Did the Sun rise north of east? South of east? Or true east (90 degrees from north)? Record the date and direction of sunrise in your notebook.

3. Repeat the experiment as the Sun sets. Record the date and direction of sunset in your notebook. Did the Sun set north of west? South of west? Or true west (270 degrees from north)?

4. If possible, repeat this experiment at least once a month for a year. What do you conclude about the direction of sunrise and sunset over the course of a year?

You Will Need

- **north-south line in your observatory**
- **horizontal angle-measuring instrument**
- **stick**

IDEAS FOR YOUR SCIENCE FAIR

- Record the time of sunrise and the time of sunset as the seasons pass. How can you explain these time changes?

- Plot a graph of time of sunrise vs. time in days and months. Plot a similar graph for sunset vs. time. Try to explain unexpected parts of your graphs, such as sunrise times for late December through January.

MAPPING THE SUN'S PATH ACROSS THE SKY

1. **On a clear night, look up at the sky** as you stand in your outdoor observatory. Imagine yourself at the center of a giant dome. Stars glisten like tiny lights set in the surface of the dome. Astronomers call this dome the celestial hemisphere. Someone on the opposite side of the earth sees the other celestial hemisphere. Together, the two celestial hemispheres make up the celestial sphere. During daytime, on a clear day, the celestial hemisphere resembles a giant blue dome.

   The stars, Moon, planets, and our own special star, the Sun, move across the celestial hemisphere every day. You can map the Sun's path across this hemisphere

You Will Need

- **clear weather**
- **your outdoor observatory**
- **clear plastic dome (hemisphere) or a large fine-mesh kitchen strainer (domes can be found on squirrel-proof bird feeders; science supply companies sell them as part of a globe kit)**
- **board or a sheet of heavy cardboard**
- **pencil**
- **marking pen**
- **tape**
- **clock or watch**
- **colored round-headed map pins (if you use a strainer)**
- **yarn**

quite easily. A clear plastic dome or a large fine-mesh kitchen strainer can represent the celestial hemisphere.

2. Put the dome or strainer on a board or a sheet of heavy cardboard. Mark the outline of its base with a pencil. Then remove the hemisphere and mark the center of the circle you drew with a dark dot. The dot represents you at the center of the celestial hemisphere. Put the dome or strainer back in its original position and tape it to its wooden or cardboard base.

3. Place the hemisphere and base in your observatory where it will be in the Sun all day. Be sure the base is level. Mark the outline of the base so that if it is accidentally moved it can be replaced in its exact position. Use the north–south line in your observatory to orient the dome. Mark an "N" on the north-facing part of the board or cardboard so that you can always put it in the same position when you repeat this experiment at a later date.

4. Begin the experiment on a clear day as early after sunrise as possible. Continue the experiment until sunset. If you use a clear dome, you can mark the Sun's position in the sky with a marking pen. Place the tip of the marking pen on the

ASTRONOMY PROJECTS WITH AN OBSERVATORY YOU CAN BUILD

dome so that the tip's shadow falls on the dot you marked at the dome's center. The mark you make will be in line with the Sun and the center dot, which represents you. It will map the Sun's position in the sky, on the celestial hemisphere (see Figure 14).

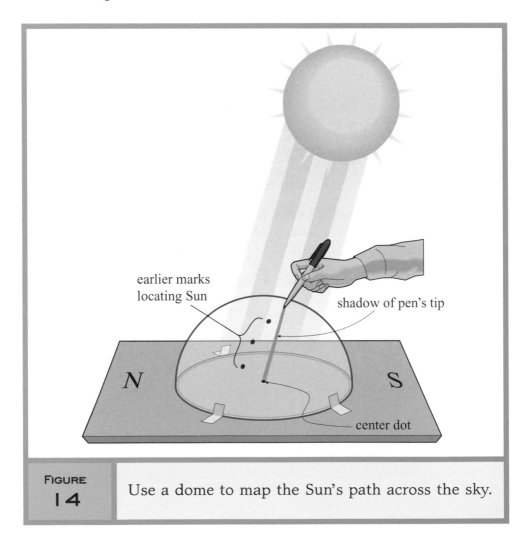

FIGURE 14   Use a dome to map the Sun's path across the sky.

76

5. Mark the Sun's position every hour or so during the time the Sun is in the sky. By the end of the day, you will have a permanent map of the Sun's path across the celestial hemisphere on that day of the year.

6. If you use a strainer, colored round-headed map pins can be used to cast their shadows on the center dot. Leave the pins in the strainer. At the end of the day, you will have a colorful map of the Sun's path across the sky. Run a piece of yarn through the pin positions as you remove them. You will then have a permanent map of the Sun's path for a particular day.

Try to do this experiment at least four times, around the 21st of March, June, September, and December. In that way you will have the highest, lowest, and middle paths of the Sun for an entire year.

When is the Sun's path highest and longest across the sky? When is its path lowest and shortest? At what latitudes is the Sun directly overhead on these dates? Repeat Experiment 2-3 to find out.

SEASONS AND THE ALTITUDE OF THE MIDDAY SUN

From your measurements of the Sun's path across the sky, you can see that the Sun's midday altitude changes from season to season. But what is the Sun's midday altitude where you live on or near the first day of a season (the 21st of March, June, September, or December)?

1. To find out, determine the time of midday (see Experiment 2-4). Next, locate a flat surface, such as your observatory (if level), a wooden deck, a flat path or driveway, or similar surface, in a sunny place. Have a partner hold a pointed stick about a meter (3 feet) long in a vertical position. A carpenter's level will help in determining when the stick is vertical. Measure the stick's height with a meterstick or tape measure. At midday, measure the length of the vertical stick's shadow.

You Will Need

- **local newspaper**
- **a flat surface in a sunny place**
- **a partner**
- **pointed stick about a meter (3 feet) long**
- **carpenter's level**
- **meterstick or tape measure**
- **paper**
- **sharp pencil**
- **ruler**
- **protractor**

2. Use your measurements to make a scaled drawing of the stick and its shadow, as shown in Figure 10. Use a protractor to measure angle *x*, which is the Sun's altitude at midday. What is the Sun's altitude at your latitude at the beginning of the season?

3. If possible, repeat this experiment at the beginning of each of the other three seasons.

IDEAS FOR YOUR SCIENCE FAIR

•   Figure out a way to make a direct measurement of the Sun's altitude from the stick and its shadow. **Remember, never look directly at the Sun; it can damage your eyes!**

•   Measure the Sun's midday altitude as often as possible for an entire year. Use the data you collect to plot a graph of the Sun's midday altitude vs. time as measured in days and months. What does your graph look like?

SEASONS AND THE SUN

After doing the previous two experiments, you know that the Sun strikes Earth at a higher angle on the first day of summer than at any other time of the year. In the winter, the Sun is low in the sky, and its light falls on Earth at a low angle.

1. To see what effect the seasonal path of the Sun has on the heat it delivers to Earth's surface, place a sheet of paper on a table in a dark room. The paper represents a portion of Earth's surface.

2. Shine a flashlight directly down on the paper. Now, tip the flashlight so that its light strikes the paper at a much lower angle, as shown in Figure 15. What happens to the area covered by the light from the flashlight? How has the amount of light per area changed? How will this affect the quantity of warmth delivered to this part of Earth?

3. Replace the paper with a globe. At the beginning of winter in the northern

You Will Need

- **sheet of paper**
- **table**
- **flashlight**
- **globe**
- **dark room**

hemisphere (around December 21), the Sun will be directly over the tropic of Capricorn (at latitude 23.5 degrees south of the equator). Hold the flashlight so that it shines straight down on the tropic of Capricorn. Slowly

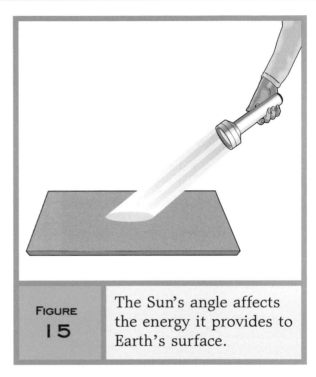

| FIGURE 15 | The Sun's angle affects the energy it provides to Earth's surface. |

move the flashlight upward, keeping it tilted at the same angle, until the light shines on the United States. What happens to the light shining on the globe? Does the light cover more, the same, or less area than it did when it was shining on the tropic of Capricorn? The Sun's light is the energy that heats Earth. How will the Sun's energy delivered to the United States compare with the heat delivered to the same area along the tropic of Capricorn on December 21?

THE EFFECT OF ANGLE ON THE ABSORPTION OF RADIANT ENERGY

1. **For a more direct measurement** of the effect of angle on the heat delivered by light, you will need three identical thermometers with a range of approximately −10 to 50°C, or 10° to 120°F.

   Prepare a black pocket for each thermometer by cutting rectangles from construction paper. The pocket will cover the lower part of the thermometer, as shown in Figure 16a. The pocket should completely cover the thermometer bulb and the lower part of the thermometer. It can be stapled as shown.

2. Put the three thermometers at equal distances from a heat lamp, as shown in Figure 16b. One thermometer should lie flat. Light will strike it at 90 degrees. A second

You Will Need

- **3 identical alcohol-based thermometers (−10 to 50°C, or 10° to 120°F)**

- **black construction paper**

- **scissors**

- **stapler**

- **heat lamp or reflector light and clamp with 75-watt bulb**

- **ruler**

- **books to prop thermometers**

- **clock or watch**

a)

thermometer

black paper

staples

b)

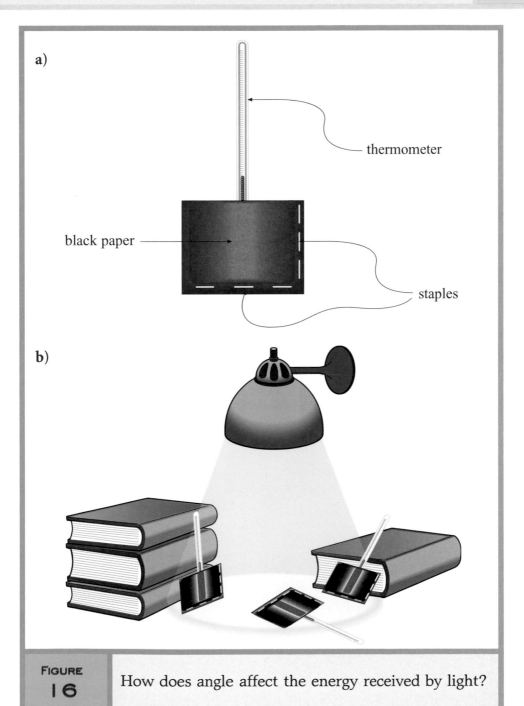

FIGURE
16

How does angle affect the energy received by light?

should be parallel to the light beam. Light will strike it at 0 degrees. The third thermometer should be at an angle of about 45 degrees to the light. Center the light over the thermometers at a height of about 30 cm (12 in).

3. All three thermometers should read approximately the same temperature when you turn on the light. Watch the temperature on the flat thermometer. Turn off the lamp after 15 minutes or before the thermometer reaches the end of its temperature range. Then immediately read and record the three temperatures.

Which thermometer showed the greatest increase in temperature? Which thermometer showed the least increase in temperature? Do your results confirm what you observed in the previous experiment?

MEASURING TIME WITH THE SUN

Early Egyptians used the Sun to measure time. You can do something similar.

1. Find a sheet of corrugated cardboard at least 40 cm (16 in) on each side. Tape a sheet of paper to the cardboard. Push a long finishing nail into the cardboard. The nail should be perpendicular to the paper and near the center of one edge.

2. Put the cardboard outdoors on a sunny, level place shortly after sunrise. Orient the cardboard so that the side with the nail is facing south. Use a pencil to mark the nail's shadow on the paper. Do this every hour until sunset. Label each shadow you mark with the time you read on a watch or clock. Mark the outline of the cardboard so that you can put it back in the same place at a later date.

3. After several days, replace the cardboard and compare

 You Will Need

- **sheet of thick corrugated cardboard at least 40 cm (16 in) on each side**

- **tape**

- **sheet of paper**

- **large finishing nail**

- **sunny, level place outdoors**

- **pencil**

- **watch or clock**

the times on your sun clock with the times on your watch or clock. Do the times still agree? Do they agree after a week? After a month? After several months?

IDEA FOR YOUR SCIENCE FAIR

Build a sundial using a gnomon. The angle (steepness) of the gnomon should match your latitude. Is it a more accurate timer than the sun clock you made?

E arly Egyptians used a sun clock like the one you made. As you found, the sun clock is not very accurate. Its time did not agree with your watch or clock time for very long. This is because the Sun's speed along its orbit changes, it rises and sets at different times as seasons change, and, as you are finding, the Sun's path across the sky changes. When Earth's north pole is tilted toward the Sun (summer in the northern hemisphere), the Sun's path across the sky is higher. When Earth is on the other side of its orbit about the Sun, its north pole tilts away from the Sun (winter in the northern hemisphere). The Sun follows a lower path across the sky.

Our clocks measure what is called the mean solar day. A mean solar day is the average time that it takes for Earth to rotate

You Will Need

- **cardboard**
- **south-facing window**
- **tape**
- **sheet of paper**
- **table or counter**
- **nail**
- **ruler**
- **clock or watch set to radio time**
- **marking pen**
- **globe**

from one midday to the next. Because the time from one midday to the next can change, the time of midday according to the Sun does not always agree with 12 o'clock noon on a clock.

To see that this is true, you can map the Sun at exactly the same clock time every few days for a month.

1. Cover the bottom of a south-facing window with cardboard. Tape a sheet of paper to a table or counter next to the bottom of the cardboard. Using a nail, make a hole through the cardboard about 10 cm (4 in.) above the paper.

2. On clear days, the Sun's image will appear as a bright spot on the paper. Set your clock or watch according to a radio time signal. At exactly noon, clock time, mark the center of the bright spot on the paper with a marking pen. Do this at exactly 12 o'clock noon at least once a week, or more often.

3. If possible, do this for a year. After a few months, you will see a pattern develop. After a year, your dots will form a figure eight. You will see that it is similar to the analemma found on globes (usually in the vicinity of the equator on the southern Pacific Ocean).

Why do you think the noontime spot moves farther from

the window during the winter and closer during the summer? As you can see, the spots you marked do not form a straight north–south line. What does this tell you about the Sun's position in the sky? During which times of the year is sun time ahead of the clock (mean solar) time? During which times is sun time behind clock time? How can you estimate how many minutes sun time is ahead of or behind clock time? Do your estimates agree with those on an analemma?

IDEA FOR YOUR SCIENCE FAIR

Figure out a way to make an analemma on a vertical surface.

DISTANCE TO THE SUN

Aristarchus of Samos estimated the distance to the Sun. He had already estimated the size of the Moon and its distance from Earth. He knew that when the Moon was exactly at first quarter, the angle from Earth to Moon to Sun must be 90 degrees, as shown in Figure 17. By measuring the angle between the Moon and the Sun (angle MES) in this right triangle, he estimated the distance to the Sun. He found the angle to be 87 degrees. Using trigonometry, he estimated

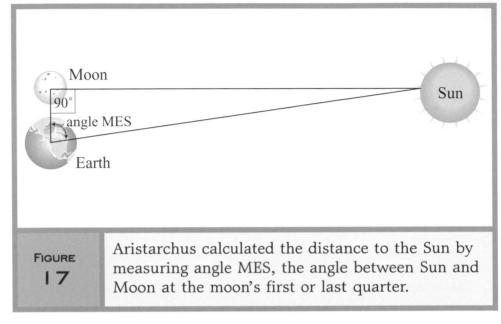

FIGURE 17	Aristarchus calculated the distance to the Sun by measuring angle MES, the angle between Sun and Moon at the moon's first or last quarter.

the distance to the Sun to be about 20 times farther than the distance to the Moon.

Today we know that angle MES is approximately 89.85 degrees, so we know the Sun is about 400 times farther from Earth than the Moon is. Knowing that the Sun is about 150,000,000 km from Earth, you can easily measure its diameter. You can do that in the next experiment.

1. **On a bright, sunny day,** find a leafy tree that provides lots of shade. If you look under the tree, you will see many small circles. These circles are called sun dapples. They are images of the Sun.

2. We can use the Sun's image to measure its diameter. Use a pin to make a small hole through the center of a file card. Tape a second file card to the end of a meterstick or yardstick. **Never look directly at the sun. It can damage your eyes!** The card taped to the end of the stick can serve as a screen on which you can make an image of the Sun. To make the image, move the card with the pinhole along the stick between the Sun and the card at the end of the stick.

3. When you have a sharp

 You Will Need

- **bright, sunny day**
- **pin with a large diameter, such as a T-pin**
- **2 file cards**
- **tape**
- **meterstick or yardstick**
- **ruler**
- **a partner**
- **paper and pencil**
- **calculator (optional)**

image of the Sun, ask a partner to place a ruler on the image (see Figure 18a). What is the diameter, in centimeters (or inches), of the Sun's image? How far, in centimeters (or inches), is the image from the pinhole? Record both the size of the image and the distance between the image and the pinhole.

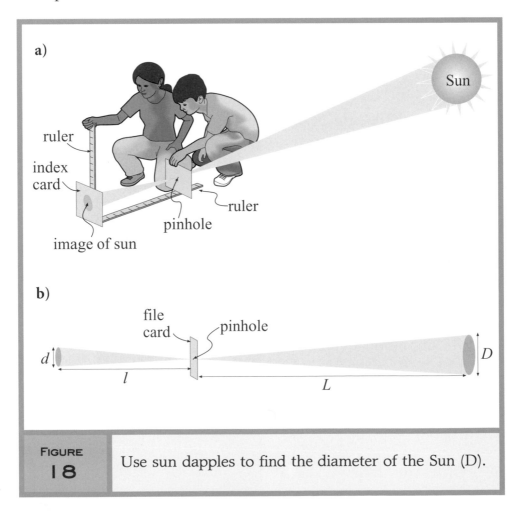

a)

ruler

index card

image of sun

pinhole

ruler

Sun

b)

file card

pinhole

d

l

L

D

| FIGURE 18 | Use sun dapples to find the diameter of the Sun (D). |

Figure 18b shows two triangles. The smaller triangle has the pinhole as its apex and the diameter of the Sun's image as its base. It is similar to the larger triangle, which also has the pinhole as its apex, but its base is the diameter of the Sun. Because these two triangles are similar (have equal angles), their sides are in the same ratio. That is:

$$\frac{D}{L} = \frac{d}{l}, \quad \text{or} \quad D = \frac{d}{l} \times L$$

L is the distance to the Sun, which we know is 150,000,000 km, and *D* represents the diameter of the Sun, which we want to find. In the little triangle, *l* is the distance from the pinhole to the Sun's image, and *d* is the diameter of the Sun's image. As the equation shows, we can find the Sun's diameter by simply multiplying $\frac{d}{l}$ by *L*. For example, the author found that the diameter of the Sun's image (*d*) was 0.5 cm when the distance from the pinhole to the image was 50 cm. Knowing the distance to the Sun was 150,000,000 km, he solved for *D* and found that

$$D = \frac{0.5 \text{ cm}}{50 \text{ cm}} \times 150{,}000{,}000 \text{ km} = 1{,}500{,}000 \text{ km}$$

What is the diameter of the Sun according to your measurements and calculation?

What happens to the size of the Sun's image if you move the screen closer to the pinhole? Can you explain why?

IDEAS FOR YOUR SCIENCE FAIR

- How can you explain the sun dapples you saw under the shade tree?

- What do you see if you make a second pinhole in the card? A third? How can you make a set of sun dapples?

STARS AND PLANETS

The word *planet* comes from a Greek word meaning "wanderer." Most of the stars you see in the sky remain in fixed positions relative to one another, but early astronomers noticed that several "stars," unlike the many others, seemed to move in relation to the fixed stars. They called these stars wanderers.

Today we know that the "wanderers" are the planets Mercury, Venus, Mars, Jupiter, and Saturn. The other close planets were discovered much later: Uranus in 1781, Neptune in 1846, and the dwarf planet Pluto in 1930.

Actually, the stars do move relative to one another, but they are so far away that their motions are difficult to detect. Our Sun is a star and it appears to move across our sky every day. Of course, it is Earth's rotation that makes the Sun appear to move from east to west every day. But do the more distant stars also appear to move?

DO STARS APPEAR TO MOVE?

1. **Go outside early in the evening** shortly after dark. Locate a group of stars you can identify in the eastern sky. Note their position relative to some landmark. Measure their altitude with your fists or your astrolabe. Also note the place where you are standing.

2. Return to the same place at one-hour intervals to look at the same stars until you go to bed. Each time, stand in the same place as before and locate your landmark. Then look for the same group of stars. Have the stars appeared to move? Has their altitude changed? If they appear to have moved, in which direction did they move?

3. Repeat this experiment with other groups of stars. Do they appear to move? If they do, in which direction do they move?

4. A month later, at the same time in the evening, stand in the same place as before and locate your landmark. Then look for the same group of stars. Are they where they

You Will Need

- **group of stars you can identify in the eastern sky**

- **a landmark**

- **astrolabe**

- **a calendar**

were before or have they moved? If they have moved, in which direction did they move?

5. Repeat this experiment at the same clock time at one-month intervals. Are the stars always in the same place at the same time? If not, in which direction have they moved?

IDEAS FOR YOUR SCIENCE FAIR

• What is the Zodiac? Locate and illustrate the constellations along the Zodiac.

• What is the ecliptic and how is it related to the Zodiac?

WHAT MOVES?
SOME OF ASTRONOMY'S HISTORY

You have observed the Sun, Moon, and stars moving from east to west across the sky or around Polaris. But what moves? Does Earth rotate and make the sky appear to turn, or does the sky and all that it holds move around Earth? Or is it all moving?

We know that Earth turns, but for thousands of years most astronomers (with the exception of a few like Aristarchus) and almost everyone else believed that Earth was the center of the universe. They were convinced that everything else—Sun, Moon, planets, stars—circled Earth. And there was good evidence for this model of the universe. The evidence included

(1) Common sense—anyone could see that everything in the sky moves around us.

(2) We, standing on Earth, do not feel any motion, so how can we be turning?

(3) It seemed logical to think that everything would fall toward the center of the universe, and all objects fall toward Earth.

(4) There was (at that time) no evidence of parallax among the stars. That is, the stars did not appear to shift relative to one another. If Earth were moving around the Sun, we would expect to see parallax among the stars; that is, the nearer stars would appear to shift relative to the more distant stars.

To see what is meant by parallax, hold one index finger close to your face. Hold your other index finger at arm's length. Look at your two fingers, first with your right eye closed, and then with your left eye closed. You will see the nearer finger shift relative to the more distant finger. Both fingers will shift relative to objects farther away.

If Earth traveled around the Sun, what would we expect to see when Earth was at opposite sides of its orbit? A near star almost in line with a more distant star in June would no longer be in line by January. They would appear to show parallax, just as your fingers did when you viewed them from your left and then your right eye.

(5) There was very good evidence to support the idea that the planets moved along circular paths around Earth. Philosophers and astronomers since the time of Plato (428–347 B.C.) believed that the circle was the perfect path for planets and stars to follow. Astronomers had shown that their observations of the movement of the planets could be explained if the planets followed circular paths around Earth. However, to make the circular motion fit their observations, they had to add smaller circles, called epicycles, to the basic and larger circular paths. This can be best understood by their explanations for retrograde motion.

(6) The retrograde movement of the planets is how they occasionally appear to move backward, as shown in Figure 19a.

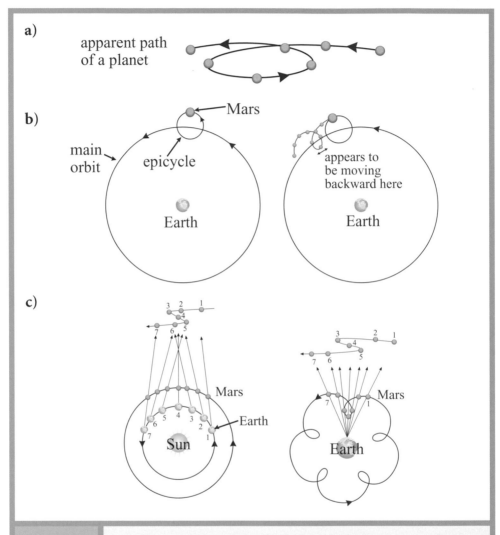

FIGURE 19

a) Retrograde motion. b) A planet moving along an epicycle while traveling along its main orbit can result in retrograde motion. c) Copernicus's Sun-centered system explains Mars' retrograde motion in a less complex way. It is simply due to the difference in the planets' velocities along their orbits around the Sun. The Earth-centered explanation is more complicated.

These early astronomers explained retrograde motion by adding epicycles to the planets' major circular orbits about Earth (Figure 19b). This led to very complicated motions. For some of the planets, multiple epicycles had to be added to make their orbits fit the observations.

Polish astronomer Nicolaus Copernicus (1473–1543) developed a Sun-centered model in which all the planets circled the Sun. His book, *On the Revolution of the Heavenly Spheres,* was published in 1543, just before he died. Copernicus had delayed the publication of his model because he knew he would be criticized by other astronomers and by the Church.

The major advantage of Copernicus's model was its simplicity. It did not require epicycles to explain retrograde motion. The slower-moving planets beyond Earth sometimes appeared to move backward against the background of the distant stars simply because they moved slower than Earth (see Figure 19c). Copernicus's model with its circular orbits did not, however, provide a better explanation of the data. Circular orbits still did not quite work unless epicycles were added.

A major breakthrough occurred in 1609 when Johannes Kepler (1571–1630), using the precise observational data of Tycho Brahe (1546–1601), another astronomer, carefully plotted the paths of the planets. He found that while the planets' orbits were nearly circular, they were not perfect circles. They were actually ellipses.

Additional evidence that Copernicus was right about the Sun being at the center of the solar system came in 1838 when Friedrich Wilhelm Bessel (1784–1846) announced that he had measured the parallax of a star.

1. **To see how an elliptical orbit differs** from a circular orbit, you can draw an ellipse. To make an ellipse, put a sheet of paper on a piece of corrugated cardboard. Near the center of the paper, insert two pins about 10 cm (4 in) apart. Cut a piece of string about 20 cm (8 in) long. Tie the ends of the string together.

2. Place the string over the two pins. Using a pencil, keep the string taut as you move the pencil around the pins to draw an ellipse (Figure 20a). The ellipse you have drawn is probably more elliptical than Earth's orbit, which is nearly circular. However, it is less elliptical than the paths of many of the comets that also orbit the Sun.

   The two pins you used to draw the ellipse are called the foci of the ellipse. As you can see from the way you drew the ellipse, all the points on the ellipse are the sum of the distances from the two foci.

You Will Need

- **paper**
- **corrugated cardboard**
- **2 pins**
- **ruler**
- **string**
- **scissors**
- **pencil**

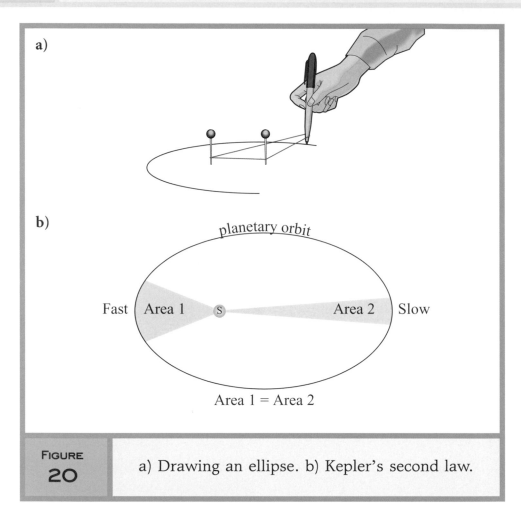

a)

b)

planetary orbit

Fast | Area 1 | S | Area 2 | Slow

Area 1 = Area 2

FIGURE
20

a) Drawing an ellipse. b) Kepler's second law.

(The length of the string from the foci to the pencil is constant.)

The Sun is located at one of the foci of Earth's orbit. When Earth is close to that focus, it moves faster; when it is farther from that focus, it moves slower. Kepler was able to show that a line connecting a planet with the Sun sweeps out equal areas in equal times. This is known as Kepler's second law (Figure 20b). His third law states that for all the planets orbiting the Sun, the cube of a planet's average distance from the Sun (R) divided by the square of its period (T, time to make one orbit) is a constant; that is:

$$\frac{R^3}{T^2} = \text{constant}$$

IDEA FOR YOUR SCIENCE FAIR

Record the mean radius of all the planets' orbits and their periods (time to make one revolution). Using a calculator, confirm Kepler's third law (R^3/T^2 = constant).

PROOF THAT EARTH ROTATES

By 1851, almost everyone was convinced that Earth, not the sky, turned (rotated); however, there was no definite proof that this was true. In that year, Jean Foucault (1819–1868), a French physician and physicist, proved that Earth indeed rotates.

Foucault knew that a pendulum follows a back-and-forth motion that does not change its direction. He built a pendulum with a very heavy bob and suspended it from a Paris church tower using a steel wire 61 m (200 ft) long. To be sure that nothing would divert the pendulum's path, he set the pendulum in motion by burning a cord that held the bob to one side. A spike attached to the bottom of the bob left a mark in dry sand as it slowly swung back and forth. Its period was nearly 16 seconds. As hours passed, the marks left in the sand slowly shifted. Earth was rotating beneath the pendulum. The pendulum's marks turned about 270 degrees during 24 hours, the angle Foucault had predicted for Paris, which is located at a latitude of about 49 degrees. At the North Pole, the path marks would turn 360 degrees in 24 hours. At the equator, they would not appear to turn at all.

Suppose you set a pendulum in motion along an east–west line at the North Pole. The pendulum would continue to move from east to west, but Earth would turn beneath it. The pendulum's swing path would appear to turn clockwise as Earth turned counterclockwise beneath it.

Now think of the same pendulum swinging along an east–west line at the equator. Earth turns from west to east beneath it, so there would be no apparent rotation of the pendulum.

1. **You can make a simple model** of Foucault's pendulum at the North Pole. Use thread to suspend a small pendulum with a Ping-Pong ball bob from a cardboard frame. Tape the bottom of the frame to a

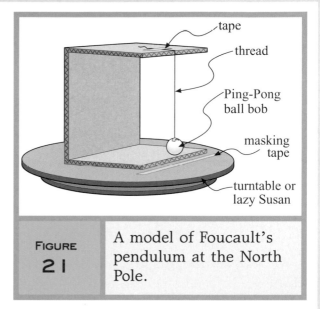

| FIGURE 21 | A model of Foucault's pendulum at the North Pole. |

turntable or lazy Susan (see Figure 21). The center of the turntable or lazy Susan represents the North Pole.

2. Use a piece of masking tape to mark the pendulum's path. Set the pendulum swinging along the path marked by the tape. Then slowly turn the turntable or lazy Susan. Can you see that the pendulum appears to rotate slowly in the opposite direction?

You Will Need

- **corrugated cardboard**
- **thread**
- **scissors**
- **Ping-Pong ball**
- **tape**
- **turntable or lazy Susan**
- **masking tape**

HOW MANY STARS CAN YOU SEE?

D**o this experiment on a clear,** cloudless night in a place that is away from any lights such as street or city lights.

You have probably heard someone say, "I can see millions of stars in the sky tonight!" It is true that there are millions— in fact, billions—of stars, but can we see millions of stars in the sky? Here is a way to find out.

1. Use scissors to cut out a square 10 cm x 10 cm from a piece of cardboard. Tape the cardboard to a ruler exactly 27.5 cm from the end of the ruler. Hold the ruler next to your eye. When you look through the square 27.5 cm away, you will see a region of the sky that is 20° x 20°. To see that this is true, draw a straight line 27.5 cm long. At one end of the line, draw a line 10 cm long perpendicular to the longer line. Then connect the ends of the two lines to make a right triangle.

You Will Need

- **clear, cloudless night in a place away from any lights**
- **cardboard**
- **scissors**
- **metric ruler**
- **tape**
- **pencil**
- **paper**
- **protractor**

2. Measure the smallest angle of the triangle with a protractor. It represents the vertical angle of sky that you will see through the square.

3. Count the number of stars you see through the square. Do this for at least 10 different parts of the sky. Record the number you count for each of the 10 samples. Then add all the stars you have counted and divide by 10. This will give you an average count for 400 square degrees of sky. In the entire sky's hemisphere, there are 20,626 square degrees. To make the best estimate of the total number of stars in the sky, multiply your average number for 400 square degrees by 51.6, because

$$20,626 \div 400 = 51.6$$

What do you find is the total number of visible stars? Is it close to a million?

USING A STAR TO FIND YOUR LATITUDE

1. **Locate Polaris (the North Star).** If you have not measured its altitude before, use your astrolabe to do so. The altitude of Polaris, in degrees, is your latitude.

2. Use a map or globe and Figure 22 to confirm the fact that the altitude of Polaris at any latitude in the northern hemisphere equals the latitude at which the altitude is measured.

3. Longitude is measured from a line called the prime meridian that runs from the North Pole, through Greenwich, England, over the equator, and on to the South Pole. You can find this meridian on a globe. It is defined to be 0 degrees longitude. Because it takes 24 hours for the Sun to appear to move 360 degrees and circle our planet, we divide 360 degrees by 24 hours:

$$\frac{360°}{24 \text{ hr}} = \frac{15°}{\text{hr}}$$

This tells us that Earth turns 15 degrees per hour.

Time zones are 15 degrees apart. If you live in a time zone between 75 and 90 degrees west of Greenwich,

You Will Need

- **astrolabe**
- **world map or globe**

your clocks will be 5 hours behind Greenwich time. When it is 12:00 noon in Greenwich, it will be 7:00 A.M. according to your clock.

4. To estimate your longitude, you need to know the time in Greenwich, England, when it is midday at your longitude. Suppose you find midday to be at 12:30 P.M. when it is 8:00 P.M. in Greenwich. You are 7.5 hours or 112.5° west of Greenwich. If your latitude is 36°, you are somewhere near Grand Canyon, Arizona.

IDEA FOR YOUR SCIENCE FAIR

If you travel a significant distance north or south of your home latitude, take your astrolabe with you. Use it to measure the altitude of Polaris and, therefore, the latitude to which you have traveled.

LIGHT FROM AFAR

We know that **Polaris** is almost directly above Earth's North Pole. But in Figure 22 it is assumed that the light coming to any latitude from Polaris is parallel to the light that goes to the North Pole. Is that a good assumption?

1. Stick three pins, several centimeters apart, into a piece of corrugated cardboard.

2. Find a clear lightbulb that has a straight filament. Screw the clear bulb into a lamp socket and plug the cord from the socket into an electrical outlet. Turn out all other lights so that the bulb with the straight filament is the only light in the otherwise dark room. Arrange the bulb so that when you look at the end of its straight filament you see a point of light, the same thing you see when you look at a star.

3. Hold the cardboard with the three pins near the point of light. Look at the shadows cast by the

You Will Need

- **3 straight pins**
- **corrugated cardboard**
- **clear 60-watt lightbulb with a straight filament**
- **lamp socket and cord**
- **dark room**
- **Sun**
- **Moon**

pins. Are the shadows parallel or do they spread apart?

4. Slowly move the cardboard away from the light. What happens to the shadows? At a large distance from the light, do the shadows appear to be parallel? What does this tell you about the light rays coming

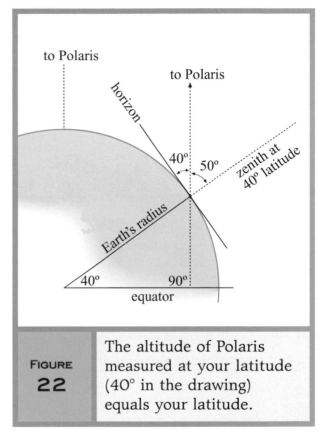

The altitude of Polaris measured at your latitude (40° in the drawing) equals your latitude.

FIGURE 22

from the point of light when you are far from the light? What does it tell you about the light that reaches Earth from a star light-years away?

5. Do you think the shadows of the pins will be parallel if you hold the cardboard in sunlight? Try it! Were you right?

6. Do you think the shadows of the pins will be parallel if you hold the cardboard in the light from a full or nearly full Moon? Try it! Were you right?

VENUS: AN EASY-TO-FIND PLANET

Venus is the brightest planet and easiest one to locate in the sky. It is usually a morning or an evening "star." When Venus is near, behind, or in front of the Sun, it cannot be seen. The Sun's brightness obscures it. When it is in any other position along its orbit, you can see it either in the eastern sky before sunrise or in the western sky after sunset. Because it is so bright, it is easy to find. If it is the evening star, it will be the first "star" to appear in the sky after sunset.

1. Your local newspaper probably gives the rising and setting times of Venus as well as of the other planets. If not, look for this information in an almanac or on the Internet.

You Will Need

- **rising and setting times for Venus (from newspaper, almanac, or Internet)**

- **your fists or the astrolabe**

- **binoculars or a telescope**

- **protractor**

- **ruler**

- **sharp pencil**

2. You can map Venus's orbit. When it is the evening "star," measure its angle from the Sun immediately after sunset. **Remember, do not**

look directly at the Sun! It can cause permanent damage to your eyes. Take the sunset position of the Sun as one point and Venus as the other. Use fists or an angle-measuring instrument to obtain the angles. Do this as often as you can, perhaps every week. Stop when Venus gets close to the Sun.

3. Look at Venus occasionally through binoculars or a telescope. Does Venus appear to have phases like the Moon? How can you explain its apparent shape? Why do you never see a full Venus?

4. When Venus is the morning "star," measure its angle from the Sun just as the Sun begins to rise. Again, do this as often as possible. Stop when Venus gets very close to the Sun.

5. From your measurements, what is the largest angle you measured between Venus and the Sun? This angle, angle VES, or angle x, in Figure 23a, occurs when a line between Venus and Earth is tangent to Venus's orbit, as shown in Figure 23a. At this point, the angle EVS is 90°, so Venus, Earth, and Sun form a right triangle. At all other positions of Venus, as seen from Earth (Figures 23b and 23c), the angle EVS will be less than 90 degrees.

6. Since the distance to the Sun is about 150,000,000 km

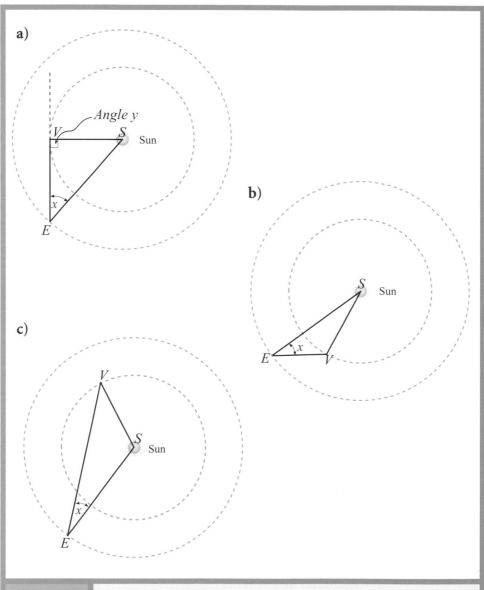

a)

b)

c)

FIGURE 23

a) Angle x (VES) is greatest when the line from Earth to Venus is tangent to Venus's orbit. At this point, position 1, angle EVS is 90°.
b) and c) At other points along Venus's orbit, angle VES is less than its maximum angle (46.3°).

(93,000,000 miles), you can find the distance between Earth and Venus. Use a protractor, ruler, and sharp pencil to make a scale drawing of the triangle in Figure 23a. Use the angle x that you measured. What is the distance between Venus and the Sun? Why is angle x never any bigger than the angle you measured?

The maximum angle between the Sun and the planet Mercury is about 23 degrees. What does this tell you about Mercury's orbit?

IDEA FOR YOUR SCIENCE FAIR

Ask an adult to help you locate the planet Mercury and measure its maximum angle from the Sun. Use that information to find the distance between Mercury and the Sun. **Remember, do not look directly at the Sun! It can cause permanent damage to your eyes.**

A MODEL TO EXPLAIN THE PHASES OF VENUS

1. **You can make a simple model** of Venus's orbit as seen from Earth. Sit in front of a glowing lightbulb in an otherwise dark room. Place a white Styrofoam ball on a pencil. Slowly move the ball around the lightbulb in front of you, as shown in Figure 24.

2. When Venus is between you and the "Sun," it reflects all the sunlight away from you, so it cannot be seen. When it is on the other side of the Sun, the Sun hides Venus. At what points in its orbit does Venus look like the Moon at first and last quarter? At what points in its orbit is Venus a crescent? At what points in its orbit do we see the most of Venus? At what points would you expect Venus to be brightest as seen from Earth? Why?

You Will Need

- **lightbulb and lamp**
- **room that can be made dark**
- **white Styrofoam ball about the size of a tennis ball**
- **pencil**

From the observations you made in Experiment 5-7, at what phase was Venus brightest? Did your observations agree with your expectations? If not, why do you think your expectations were not correct?

IDEA FOR YOUR SCIENCE FAIR

Galileo (1564–1642) used the phases of Venus to show that it orbited the Sun and not Earth. Modify the model you used in this experiment to show how the phases of Venus would be different if Venus orbited Earth.

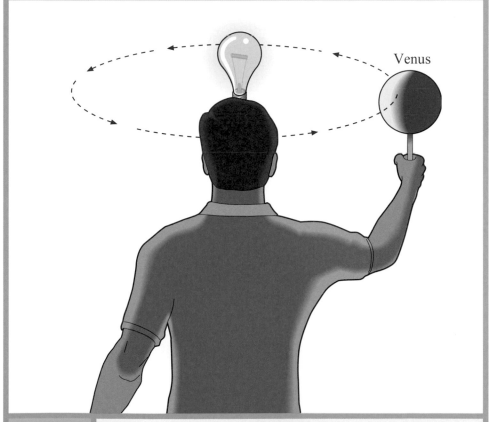

Venus

FIGURE 24	Moving a ball around a lightbulb provides a model of Venus's orbit around the Sun as seen from Earth (your head in the model).

JUPITER AND FOUR OF ITS MOONS

In 1610, Galileo turned his telescope toward the planet Jupiter. He continued to watch Jupiter for several months. What he saw convinced him that Copernicus was right—not all celestial bodies go around Earth!

1. To see what convinced Galileo, find the planet Jupiter in a clear night sky. (The position of planets in the sky can be found in most newspapers and almanacs.) Jupiter is quite bright and easy to find.

2. Look at the planet through binoculars or a telescope. Near the planet you may see four smaller bright dots. All four may not be visible at the same time. One or more may be behind or in front of the planet. Continue to watch these bright objects. They are the moons of Jupiter, often called the Galilean satellites in honor of Galileo, who discovered them. If you watch these moons several times each night, night after night, you will be able to identify them and see that they move about the planet. It will help to draw a small diagram each time

You Will Need

- **good binoculars or telescope**

you view the moons. In that way you will see how their positions change with time.

3. The period of a satellite is the time it takes that satellite to make one orbit about the planet. Try to establish the period of each of Jupiter's moons. Once you do, you will be able to identify the moons by consulting Table 2. Why would you expect your measurements of the periods of Jupiter's moons be a little different from those found in Table 2?

TABLE 2	The Galilean Satellites of Jupiter		
Moon	Period (days)	Diameter of moon (km)	Distance of moon from Jupiter (km)
Io	1.77	3,630	422,000
Europa	3.55	3,138	671,000
Gandymede	7.16	5,262	1,070,000
Callisto	16.7	4,800	1,880,000

Later, with better telescopes and space probes, astronomers discovered that Jupiter had many more smaller moons.

In Galileo's time, philosophers and theologians believed

Earth was the center of the universe. They believed that all celestial bodies circled a stationary Earth. Seeing moons going about Jupiter confirmed Galileo's belief that Copernicus was right—Earth is not the center of the universe. The planets, including Earth, orbit the Sun. And these planets, such as Jupiter, have their own moons that orbit the planet, not Earth.

IDEAS FOR YOUR SCIENCE FAIR

- An astronomical unit (1 AU) is the distance from Earth to the Sun. Figure out a way to measure the radius of Jupiter's orbit about the Sun in astronomical units.

- What is Venus's distance from the Sun in astronomical units?

- Kepler's law states that for all planets orbiting the Sun, the cube of the average radius of their orbits divided by the square of their periods is a constant; that is, $R^3/T^2 = K$. Using the data in Table 2, does Kepler's law hold for the moons orbiting Jupiter?

INNER AND OUTER PLANETS

Venus and Mercury are called the inner planets. They are closer to the Sun than Earth is. As a result, we never see them more than 46 and 23 degrees, respectively, from the Sun. When an inner planet is on the opposite side of the Sun from Earth, it is said to be at superior conjunction. When it is between Earth and Sun, it is said to be at inferior conjunction.

The outer planets, which include Mars, Jupiter, Saturn, Uranus, Neptune, Pluto, and possibly others, are farther from the Sun than Earth is. Therefore, as viewed from Earth, they can be anywhere from 0 to 180 degrees from the Sun. At 0°, when the planet is behind the Sun, the planet is said to be at conjunction. At 180°, when the planet is on the opposite side of Earth from the Sun, we say it is at opposition. Can you figure out a way to find the distance of an outer planet, such as Jupiter, from the Sun?

Arbor Scientific
P.O. Box 2750
Ann Arbor, MI 48106-2750
(800) 367-6695
http://www.arborsci.com

Carolina Biological Supply Co.
2700 York Road
Burlington, NC 27215-3398
(800) 334-5551
http://www.carolina.com

Connecticut Valley Biological Supply Co., Inc.
82 Valley Road, Box 326
Southampton, MA 01073
(800) 628-7748
http://www.ctvalleybio.com

Delta Education
P.O. Box 3000
80 Northwest Blvd.
Nashua, NH 03061-3000
(800) 258-1302
http://www.delta-education. com

Edmund Scientific
60 Pearce Avenue
Tonawanda, NY 14150-6711
(800) 728-6999
http://www.scientificsonline. com

Educational Innovations, Inc.
362 Main Avenue
Norwalk, CT 06851
(888) 912-7474
http://www.teachersource.com

Fisher Science Education
4500 Turnberry Drive
Hanover Park, IL 60133
(800) 955-1177
http://new.fishersci.com

Frey Scientific
P.O. Box 8101
100 Paragon Parkway
Mansfield, OH 44903
(800) 225-3739
http://www.freyscientific.com

Nasco-Fort Atkinson
P.O. Box 901
901 Janesville Avenue
Fort Atkinson, WI 53538-0901
(800) 558-9595
http://www.nascofa.com

Nasco-Modesto
P.O. Box 3837
4825 Stoddard Road
Modesto, CA 95352-3837
(800) 558-9595
http://www.enasco.com

Sargent-Welch/VWR Scientific
P.O. Box 4130
Buffalo, NY 14217
(800) 727-4368
http://www.SargentWelch.com

Science Kit & Boreal Laboratories
777 East Park Drive
P.O. Box 5003
Tonawanda, NY 14150
(800) 828-7777
http://www.sciencekit.com

Wards Natural Science
P.O. Box 92912
5100 West Henrietta Road
Rochester, NY 14692-9012
(800) 962-2660
http://www.wardsci.com

FURTHER READING

BOOKS

Bochinski, Julianne Blair. *More Award-Winning Science Fair Projects.* Hoboken, N.J.: John Wiley and Sons, 2004.

Dispezio, Michael A. *Super Sensational Science Fair Projects.* New York: Sterling Publishers, 2002.

Gardner, Robert. *Science Project Ideas About Space Science.* Berkeley Heights, N.J.: Enslow Publishers, Inc., 2002.

Gifford, Clive. *The Kingfisher Facts and Records Book of Space.* New York: Kingfisher, 2001.

Kerrod, Robin. *The Way the Universe Works.* New York: Dorling Kinderslcy, 2002.

Mechler, Garry (Sky Maps by Will Tirion). *National Audubon Society Field Guide/Night Sky.* New York: Scholastic, 1999.

Stott, Carole. *Astronomy.* Boston: Kingfisher, 2003.

Sudipta, Bardhan-Quallen. *Championship Science Fair Projects: 100 Sure-to-Win Experiments.* New York: Sterling, 2004.

INTERNET ADDRESSES

National Space Science Data Center
   http://nssdc.gsfc.nasa.gov

Yahooligans! Science and Nature: Astronomy and Space
   http://kids.yahoo.com/science/

INDEX